AF386532

TOM NORMAND was born in Aberdour in Fife. He was educated in Dunfermline, and subsequently took a degree in Sociology and Politics at Glasgow College. His doctoral thesis, in the Sociology of Culture, was taken at Durham University. He has taught at Duncan of Jordanstone College of Art in Dundee, and, since 1982, has lectured in the History of Art at the University of St Andrews. He has published widely in the history of British art with a special interest in developments in art and photography in Scotland. He has lectured, nationally and internationally, on Scottish art, culture and society.

PORT*f*OLIO

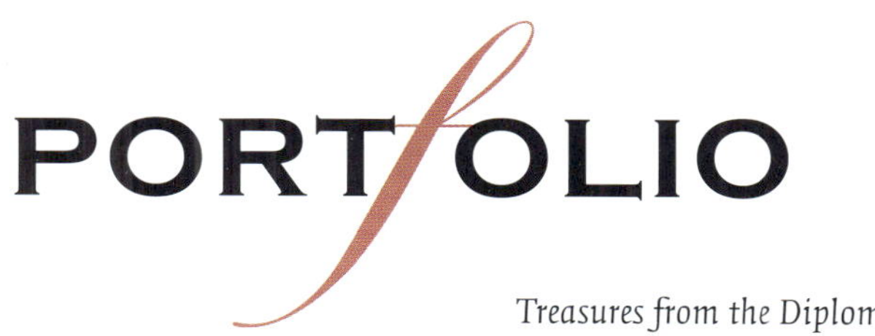

*Treasures from the Diploma Collection
at the Royal Scottish Academy*

TOM NORMAND

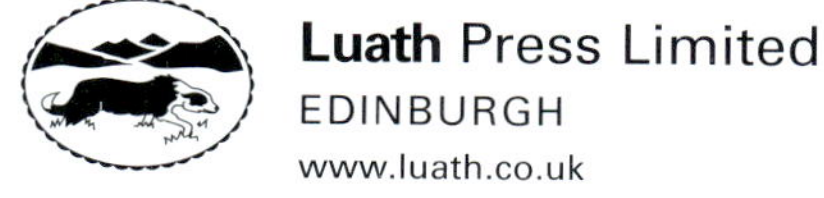

Luath Press Limited
EDINBURGH
www.luath.co.uk

First published 2013

ISBN: 978-1-908373-52-6

The paper used in this book is recyclable.
It is made from low chlorine pulps produced
in a low energy, low emissions manner from
renewable forests.

Printed and bound by Martins the Printers,
Berwick upon Tweed

Typeset in 10.5 point Quadraat
by 3btype.com

CONTENTS

Hidden in the vaults of an Edinburgh gallery there exists the 300 plus works of art that constitute the Diploma Collection of the Royal Scottish Academy of Art. These treasures represent some of the finest artworks from Scotland's artists, and recognise a history of nearly 200 years of excellence in the visual arts. Established in 1826 the Scottish Academy (designated Royal Scottish Academy in 1838) is a professional organisation, created and run by artists, that promotes the best qualities of Scotland's art. On being elected to the academy an artist confirms their status by depositing a 'diploma' work in the academy's collection. This work – a painting, sculpture, architectural design or model, print, photograph, or multi-media presentation – is offered as a symbol of the artist's finest creative invention. This book presents a selection of some of the best, and most intriguing, works from the academy's Diploma Collection. It also brings into the light the extraordinary treasures of one of Scotland's finest and most important collections of art.

This book could not have been written without the generous assistance of the Academy, its Academicians, and administrators. I am delighted to acknowledge the selfless work of the Collections Curator, Dr Joanna Soden, who has read the text and offered valuable comments – frequently saving my blushes. Dr Soden's colleague Sandy Wood, Assistant Curator, has been generous with his time and helpful with every variety of information. Also the Programme Director, Colin Greenslade, who has been positive and encouraging throughout. The Librarian to the Academy, Will Maclean, has been an ever-present *consigliere* and supportive commentator. And, the guiding presence of the previous Secretary to the Academy, and now President, Arthur Watson, has been a stabilising influence. Amongst Academicians and Honorary Academicians who have given of their thought and insight I would like to acknowledge, with thanks: William Brotherston, Joyce Cairns, Calum Colvin, Richard Demarco, Stuart Duffin, Gareth Fisher, Ronald Forbes, Marian Leven, Sandy Moffat, James Morrison, Glen Onwin, Willie Rodger, Kate Whiteford and Adrian Wiszniewski.

This book is a *selected* record of works in the academy's Diploma Collection. As such it has been neglectful of many meritorious, and indeed outstanding, works of art that are absent from the appraisal. There is a reason for these unfortunate omissions. Throughout the text I have tried to maintain a narrative thread that highlights changes of rhythm and tempo in the history of the academy's Diploma Collection, and so in the nature of Scotland's visual culture. Consequently, the selection of works included here was shaped by this guiding idea. To those eminent painters, sculptors, architects, photographers and printmakers who are not included here I offer my sincere apologies.

1 THOMAS HAMILTON
Design for the Royal High School, Edinburgh
(c.1825–31)
Watercolour, gouache and pencil on paper
Deposited 1831
Support size: 73.5 x 130cm

2 WILLIAM HENRY PLAYFAIR
Design for Surgeons' Hall, Edinburgh
(c.1829–32)
Pen, ink and wash on paper
Deposited 1836
Support size: 43 x 58cm

3 JOHN SYME
The Solicitor General, Lord Cockburn (1831).
Oil on canvas
Deposited 1831
Support size: 127 x 111.4cm

4 PATRICK GIBSON
Landscape Composition (c.1827–29)
Oil on panel
Deposited c.1829
Support size: 50.2 x 76.5cm

5 JOHN STEELL
David Scott SA (1831)
Marble
Deposited 1831
Height: 65cm. Width: 34cm. Depth: 24cm

6 DAVID SCOTT
Cain Degraded (or Remorse) (1831)
Oil on canvas
Deposited 1831
Support: 183 x 163cm

7 JAMES GILES
The Weird Wife o' Lang Stane Lea (1830)
Oil on canvas

Deposited 1831
Support size: 80 x 116.9cm

8 WILLIAM BORTHWICK JOHNSTONE
Scene at Holyrood 1566 (1855)
Oil on canvas
Deposited 1855
Support size: 86.4 x 153.7cm

9 CHARLES LEES
The Summer Moon – Bait Gatherers (1858)
Oil on canvas
Deposited 1860
Support size: 51.1 x 76.1cm

10 JOSEPH NOEL PATON
Oberon and Titania– first study for The Quarrel
(1846)
Oil on canvas
Deposited 1850
Support size: 43.6 x 64cm

11 SAMUEL BOUGH
Edinburgh from Bonnington (1875)
Oil on canvas
Deposited 1875
Support size: 45.8 x 61.1cm

12 WILLIAM FLEMING VALLANCE
Reading the War News (1881)
Oil on canvas
Deposited 1881
Support size: 50 x 76cm

13 ROBERT GIBB
The Sea King (1882)
Oil on canvas
Deposited 1882
Support size: 91.4 x 114.3cm

14 WILLIAM BEATTIE BROWN
Coire-na-Faireamh, in Applecross Deer Forest,
Ross-shire (c.1883–4)
Oil on canvas

Deposited 1884
Support size: 67.8 x 114.6cm

15 JAMES PITTENDRIGH MACGILLIVRAY
The Right Reverend Monsignor Munro
(c.1892–1901)
Bronze
Deposited 1901, Accepted 1922
Height: 34cm. Width: 19.5cm. Depth: 21cm

16 ROBERT MCGREGOR
Man goeth forth to his work and to his labour
until evening (1888)
Oil on canvas
Deposited 1889
Support size: 45.7 x 76.3cm

17 ROBERT ALEXANDER
Wat and Wearie (c.1886)
Oil on canvas
Deposited 1888
Support size: 81.9 x 122.8cm

18 JOSEPH DENOVAN ADAM
Evening, Strathspey (or The Glory of Dying
Day) (c.1891)
Oil on canvas
Deposited 1892
Support size: 136.8 x 198.1cm

19 ROBERT LORIMER
Earlshall, Fife, the house and garden as restored
1890–1894 for R W Mackenzie Esq of Earlshall
(1895)
Pen and ink on paper
Deposited 1922
Support size: 57.6 x 81.4cm

20 JAMES GUTHRIE
Midsummer (1892)
Oil on canvas
Deposited 1893
Support size: 101.8 x 126.2cm

21 EDWARD ARTHUR WALTON
The Portfolio (c.1905)
Oil on canvas
Deposited 1906
Support size: 120.7 x 98.4cm

22 JAMES PATERSON
A Dream of the Nor' Loch and Edinburgh Castle
(c.1904)
Oil on canvas
Deposited 1913
Support size: 102 x 127.5cm

23 HENRY LINTOTT
Avatar (1916)
Oil on canvas
Deposited 1923
Support size: 101.8 x 127.7cm

24 JOHN DUNCAN
Ivory, Apes and Peacocks (1923)
Tempera on canvas
Deposited 1924
Support size: 101.6 x 152.4cm

25 SAMUEL JOHN PEPLOE
Boy Reading (1921)
Oil on canvas
Deposited 1927
Support size: 76.3 x 64cm

26 FRANCIS CAMPBELL BOILEAU CADELL
The Poet (1912)
Oil on canvas
Deposited 1937
Support size: 86.4 x 111.8cm

27 WILLIAM OLIPHANT HUTCHISON
Portrait of James Gunn (1927)
Oil on canvas
Deposited 1944
Support size: 127.5 x 103cm

28 JAMES COWIE
Miss Barbara Graham Cowie (c.1938–39)
Oil on plywood
Deposited 1946
Support size: 101.8 x 68.8cm

29 ROBERT SIVELL
Portrait of Hamish Paterson (c.1934)
Oil on canvas
Deposited 1946
Support size: 106.9 x 64.7cm

30 PHYLLIS MARY BONE
Shere Khan the Tiger (1930)
Bronze (on wooden plinth)
Deposited 1944
Height: 32.9cm. Width: 96.5cm. Depth:
24.5cm

31 ANNE REDPATH
In the Chapel of St Jean, Tréboul (c.1954–6)
Oil on hardboard
Deposited 1956
Support size: 86.3 x 111.6cm

32 WILLIAM GILLIES
Still-life; Yellow Jug and Striped Cloth (c.1955)
Oil on canvas
Deposited 1956
Support size: 112 x 114.7cm

33 JOHN MAXWELL
The Bull (c.1957–61)
Oil on panel
Deposited 1962
Sight size: 58.7 x 85.8cm

34 WILLIAM MACTAGGART
At Longniddry (or After Rain, Longniddry)
(c.1938)
Oil on hardboard
Deposited 1971
Support size: 60.5 x 99.6cm

35 ROBIN PHILIPSON
Lament (1968)
Oil on canvas
Deposited 1971
Support size: 213.8 x 160.4cm

36 JOAN EARDLEY
Summer Sea (1962)
Oil on board
Deposited 1964
Support size: 122 x 183cm

37 ESME GORDON
Leeds Permanent Building Society, new branch office, Dundee (1978)
Pencil, watercolour and black and white photographs on paper
Deposited 1978
Sight size: 72.7 x 112.7cm

38 BET LOW
Green Place (c.1960–69)
Oil on hardboard
Deposited 2005
Support size: 69.5 x 58.5cm

39 FRANCES WALKER
Foreshore at Footdee (c.1980–3)
Oil on hardboard
Deposited 1983
Support size: 102.0 x 127.3cm

40 WILLIAM BROTHERSTON
Hat (Hat for Joseph Beuys) (1986)
Patinated bronze
Deposited 2006
Height: 27cm. Width: 49cm. Depth: 47cm

41 ELIZABETH BLACKADDER
Self Portrait with Cat (1976)
Oil on canvas
Deposited 1977
Support: 111.2 x 126.8cm

42 JOHN HOUSTON
Towards Skye (1975–76)
Oil on canvas
Deposited 1977
Support size: 101 x 112cm

43 DAVID MICHIE
On the Ramblas (1976)
Oil on canvas
Deposited 1977
Support size: 101.5 x 126.4cm

44 JAMES CUMMING
Table Assembly with Rusted Tins (c.1976)
Oil on canvas
Deposited 1977
Support size: 91.9 x 122cm

45 JACK KNOX
Snack in a Dutch Museum (c.1977–78)
Polyvinyl acetate on canvas
Deposited 1981
Support size: 121.5 x 152.1cm

46 BILL SCOTT
Twentieth Century Pad (c.1983)
Bronze
Deposited 1985
Height: 21.5cm. Width: 29.9cm. Depth: 29.7cm

47 ISI METZSTEIN
College at Cumbernauld (c. 1998)
Plywood, mdf, card and paint
Deposited 1999
Height 38.0 x Width 80.5 x Depth 40.6cm

48 WILL MACLEAN
Boston 'T' (1989)
Powdered metal acrylic paint on plywood
with cast acrylic and found objects
Deposited 1991
Height: 115cm. Width: 93cm. Depth: 10cm

49 JOYCE CAIRNS
Polish Journey (c.1998)
Oil on hardboard
Deposited 1999
Support size: 175.7 x 173.7cm

50 ALEXANDER MOFFAT
The Rock (The Radical Road) (1989–90)
Oil on canvas
Deposited 2009
Support size: 137 x 183cm

51 ADRIAN WISZNIEWSKI
Sculptress (c.2007)
Oil on canvas
Deposited 2007
Support size: 49 x 39.2cm

52 CALUM COLVIN
Venus Anadyomene (after Titian) (1998)
C-type photograph (unique edition 1/10)
Deposited 2007
Sight size: 150 x 120cm

53 KATE WHITEFORD
From the Red Cabinet (diptych), (c.2001)
Watercolour on parchment paper
Deposited 2007
Support size: 28.7 x 21.2cm (each)

54 MARIAN LEVEN
Weathering (c.2008)
Acrylic on canvas
Deposited 2008
Support size: 123 x 153cm

55 GLEN ONWIN
Geevor Ortus (quadtych) (1997)
Panel 1: Coal dust pigment oil paint,
paraffin wax, evaporated brine NaCl (salt)
on canvas laid on board.

Panel 2: China clay pigment oil paint,
paraffin wax, evaporated brine NaCl (salt)
on canvas laid on board.

Panel 3: Tin ore pigment oil paint, paraffin wax, evaporated brine NaCl (salt) on canvas laid on board.

Panel 4: Pottery clay pigment oil paint, paraffin wax, evaporated brine NaCl (salt) on canvas laid on board.
Deposited 2010
Support size: 122 x 99cm (each panel).

56 GARETH FISHER
Crystalobite c.2004
Plaster and mixed media
Deposited 2006
Sculpture: 28.5 x 18.5 x 21cm
Case: 40 x 40.1 x 32.1cm

57 RONALD FORBES
Diana Surprised by Actaeon (1998–2001)
Acrylic on linen
Deposited 2006
Support size: 152.5 x 183cm

58 WILLIE RODGER
Temptation and Fall (1975)
Lino woodcut on paper
Deposited 2005
Sight size: 82.5 x 56.5cm

59 STUART DUFFIN
Hope in Wisdom, Hope in Darkness (2005)
Mezzotint on paper
Deposited 2006
Support size: 50 x 89.3cm

60 JOHN BYRNE
Smoking Beach Boy (triptych)
Oil on hardboard
Deposited 2007
Support size: 122 x 91.5cm (each panel)

61 ARTHUR WATSON
Arkival (2008–)
Digital colour prints, multi-media installation, ongoing assemblage.
Deposited: ongoing

The Royal Scottish Academy of Art and Architecture may be defined through any number of its attributes and its component parts. It is, undoubtedly, an 'institution' and as such it is sometimes viewed as part of the 'establishment', as a guardian of 'tradition', and as a protector of certain, circumscribed, principles and values. This, ungenerous, characterisation might recognise the grandly neo-classical building on The Mound in Edinburgh as an exemplar of 'Academic' ideals. As such the institution may be pilloried as rule-bound and regressive, and certainly this is a common trope of a 'Modernist' construction of art history. Hence, the academy is that thing that ambitious and avant-garde artists react against. Equally, and related,

the academy – any academy – might be presented as a closed organisation serving only the interests of its members and the social network around that elect group. A sociology, or an institutional history, of academies might start from this point and would develop some fascinating studies through that theme. And, of course, an academy might be examined through the lens of economic history and here the 'professionalisation' of art and artists in the modern period would be recognised as a component part of capitalist development: artists protecting their market-place in a competitive social world. All of these are valuable approaches and they have shone a clear light on the construction of academic principles and academic values.

David Young Cameron, *The National Gallery and The Royal Scottish Academy*, 1916

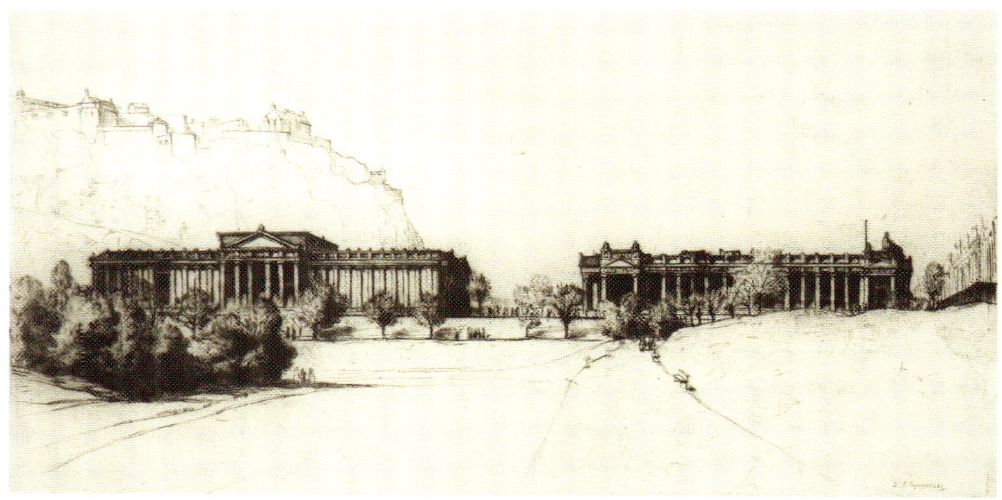

However, there is a counterpoint to these positions, and it is also possible to identify attributes within the academy – any academy – that are positive and progressive. Evidently, with the breakdown of old systems of patronage during the 18th century – a patronage gleaned from the church and the aristocracy – artists were compelled to form organisations that would protect their position and defend their interests. Indeed to create their own market-place. Extending the old guild system academies sprang up throughout Europe that were created in order to propagate, and advertise, the best qualities within the craft and art. Augmented by systems of dealerships and a developing museum and gallery culture this newly constructed art-market would become the forum for visual culture in the modern age. But there was one significant difference in relation to academies of art: they were organised, controlled and run by artists. These were juries of peers who would evaluate works of art and recognise quality and virtue. Later, in the 19th and 20th centuries, these juries would be challenged by the avant-garde who would decry the regulatory nature of academic art, but always it was artists in discourse with artists. Indeed, the avant-garde needed the academy in order to define itself as an entity and, typically, the avant-garde itself would emerge as a kind of academy. But, it is the idea of the academy as an artist-initiated and artist-led organisation that is significant for it signals a unique disposition that privileges the viewpoint of the creative worker. In this respect a defining characteristic of the academy is the recognition, the display, and the collection of art works that reflect the creative capacities of academicians.

The refurbished Royal Scottish Academy rooms, with Academicians, 1911, RSA Archives, Photographer: Francis Caird Inglis

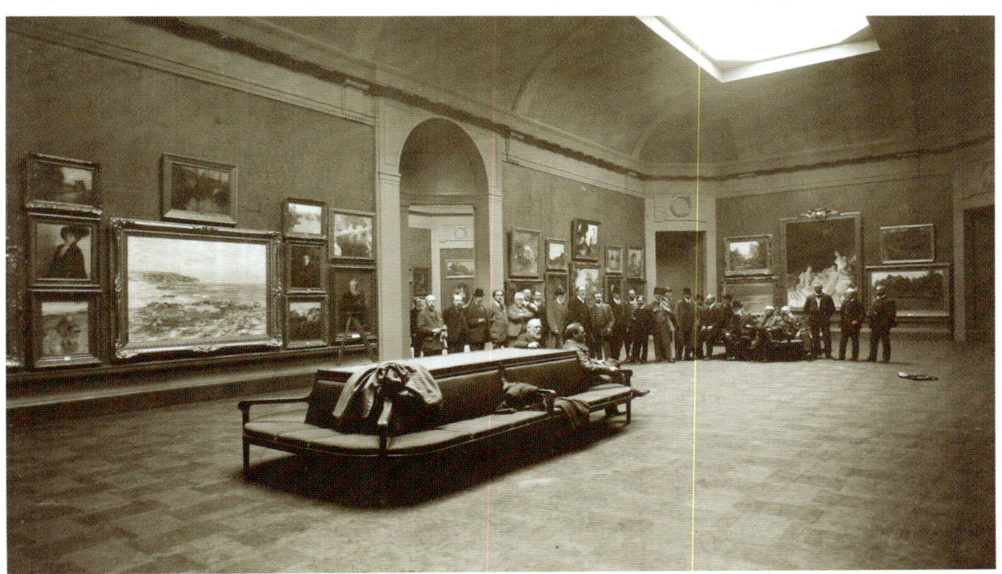

The Diploma Collection at the Royal
Scottish Academy is evidence of this
procedure, but it is much more than a
simple collection of works. It is, in some
sense, an index of the history of Scottish
art from the 1820s to the present day and
as such a representation of the quality and
character of Scotland's visual culture. The
genesis of this collection is enshrined in
the founding Constitution and Laws of the
Academy where, in the amended version of
2008, it is stated that:

> The Academician-Elect shall from time of
> Election be summoned to Assemblies of
> Academicians, and be entitled to the privi-
> leges of Membership. During the first year
> of Membership the Academician-Elect shall
> sign the Book kept by the Secretary, pay the
> subscription and deposit a Diploma work in
> the Royal Scottish Academy (to remain the
> property of the Academy) representing that
> discipline the Academician-Elect professes.
> The work proposed would first be approved
> by Council and then ratified at the next
> Assembly of Academicians
> (RSA Constitution and Laws 2008).

Consequently an academician is never fully
recognised until the diploma work has
been accepted into the collection.

There are interesting issues in respect of
this aspect of the Constitution and Laws.
In its earliest versions it was assumed that
all academicians would be men. Even as
late as 1930 the regulation read:

> 42. No Election of an Academician or
> Associate shall be deemed valid until he has
> received his Diploma, signed by the
> President and Secretary.

> 43. No Academician-Elect or Associate-Elect
> shall receive his Diploma, or be summoned
> to Assemblies of Academicians, or to the

General assemblies of the Academy respec-
tively, or be entitled to the privileges of
Membership, until he shall have signed the
Rules and the Obligation in the Book kept by
the Secretary, and paid his subscription, and
no Academician-Elect until he shall have
deposited in the Royal Scottish Academy (to
remain the property of the Academy) a
Picture, Bas-relief, Engraving, or other
specimen of his abilities, in that walk of Art
which he professes, approved of by an
Assembly of Academicians...
(RSA Constitution and Laws 1930).

Indeed the first woman to be elected a full
academician was the sculptor Phyllis Bone,
in 1944. Certainly the proprieties of
Georgian and Victorian society mitigated
against a woman occupying a professional
role, but it is the case that an artist like
Frances 'Fanny' McIan would be elected an
honorary member of the academy in 1854
and women both exhibited at the academy,
and were given associate status, from its
earliest years.

Furthermore, not all elected academicians
may be represented in the collection. In his
institutional history of 1973 Esme Gordon
notes that:

> The present day Diploma collection, if so
> large that it cannot all be exhibited simulta-
> neously, is far from complete. Disregarding
> any works due from present day members,
> 37 artists are unrepresented. Whatever the
> reasons, the lacunae range from the
> President of the day, George Watson and his
> son, a successor in office, Sir John Watson
> Gordon, a President of the Royal Academy,
> Sir Francis Grant, the two Secretaries,
> Nicholson and Hill, and 14 others of their
> contemporaries. To this list must be added
> pictures regrettably so disfigured with the
> cracks and blacks arising from the incorpo-

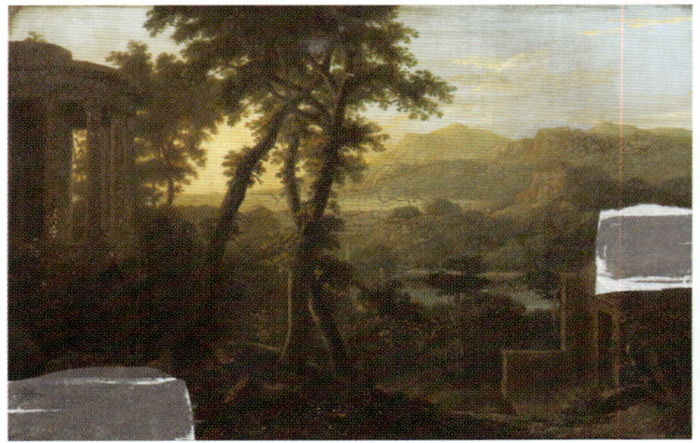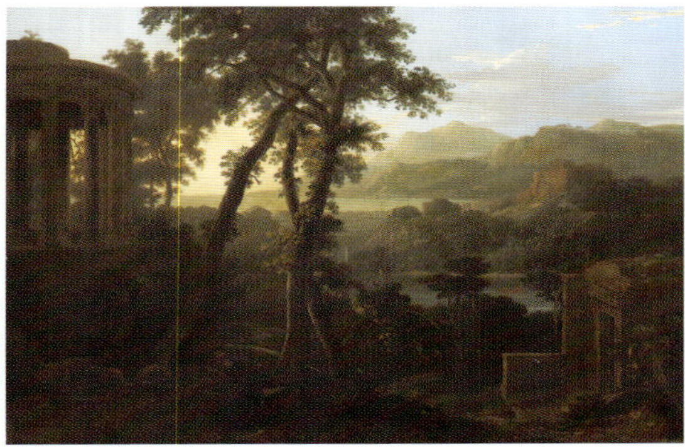

Patrick Gibson, *Landscape Composition*, c.1827–9 (before and after conservation)

ration of bitumen, that they are now completely obliterated. Amongst those withdrawn from the collection for this reason are pictures by Sir William Allan, John Zephaniah Bell, Patrick Gibson, Sir George Harvey and J. Francis Williams (Gordon 56).

Though it is the case that the research of the current Collections Curator, Dr Joanna Soden has amended these insights:

> Esme Gordon's text is rather misleading... At the time of writing his book there was still a huge amount of research to be undertaken on the collections. For example there are Diploma Works by Sir John Watson Gordon (*A Grandfather's Lesson*, c.1829, deposited 1831) and Sir Francis Grant (*Head of a Jew*, c.1823–4, deposited 1831). But I can confirm that there are no extant Diploma Works by Nicholson & Hill...
> (Soden, notes).

And, concerning the 'withdrawn' works noted by Gordon, Dr Soden comments:

> We do have the following: Sir William Allan (*The Stirrup Cup*, no date), Patrick Gibson (*Landscape Composition*, c.1826), Sir George Harvey (*The Alarm*, deposited 1831), and J Francis Williams (*Scene on the Ayrshire Coast – storm clearing off*, c.1824–7, deposited 1831) (Soden, notes).

In fact, it is the case that no diploma works were actually withdrawn from the collection in the sense of being deaccessioned, but damaged works were stored and with modern conservation techniques may be returned to the collection. Indeed, the diploma collection painting by Patrick Gibson is a case in point for the work was damaged by varnish stain, but has been recently returned to its pristine condition.

There are other idiosyncracies of the diploma collection and its regulations. While a member may be elected a full member of the academy in a given year that membership is not ratified until the diploma work has been accepted by Council and the Assembly of the Academy. Consequently a member may be elected but remain provisional for a number of years; and there are examples of academicians submitting work to the diploma collection many years after their election. Likewise there is, or has been until the revision of the constitution in 2005, a strict residency qualification. To become an elected member of the Royal Scottish Academy an individual need not be Scottish, but it has been expected that the larger part of their career should have been occasioned within Scotland. For this reason important figures like John Bellany are designated 'Honorary', their residency 'furth of Scotland' being a barrier to election. Moreover the radical modernisation of the Constitution, in 2005, has meant that the old designation of Associate of the Royal Scottish Academy (ARSA) has now disappeared: all ARSAs becoming full members in that year, and the election to full membership being automatic for new academicians. However, even under these conditions an academician remains RSA Elect until the diploma work is submitted and accepted.

Whatever the nuances surrounding the processes of election and the submission of a diploma work the fact remains that the diploma collection of the academy exists as a core representation of the history of art from Scotland. Certainly there have been additions and accretions to the academy's collection generally, but the diploma collection remains inviolable: it represents the essence of the academy's history and work, and exists as such in perpetuity. The selection of images that follow, and the commentary, is a snapshot of this prestigious collection. It gives, in outline, a sense of the development of the academy as an institution and the diploma collection as the manifest expression of the extraordinary creativity of Scottish art.

James Pittendrigh Macgillivray, *Design for Academician's robes*, 1911.

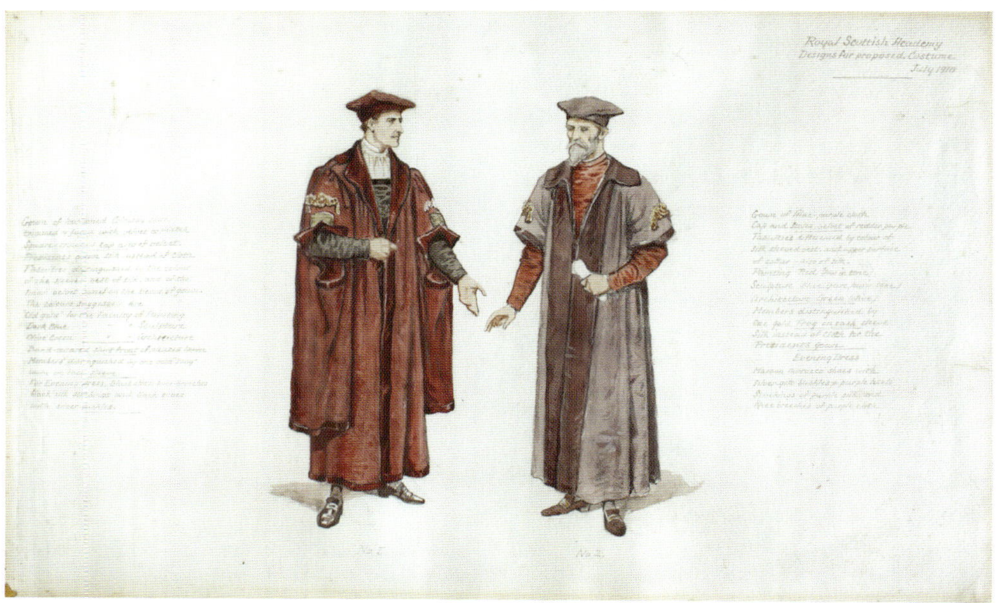

Edinburgh, famously, is two cities; an 'old' and a 'new'. The old being that medieval world that clings to the sides of the spine of rock running from the castle, high on its volcanic crag, down the High Street or 'Royal Mile' to the palace of Holyrood. The new, to the north, is the elegant neo-classical and Georgian grid, originally planned by the architect James Craig in 1766 and further developed throughout the 18th and 19th centuries.

The principal landmarks of this 'Athens of the North' were created by two eminent academicians, Thomas Hamilton and William Henry Playfair. Thomas Hamilton (1784–1858) was a founding member of the academy in 1826 and was, characteristically, from an artisanal background. Through speculative building schemes and commercial commissions, readily available in Edinburgh's expanding townscape, he grew in reputation to become a recognised master of the neo-classical manner. His diploma work, the *Design for The Royal High School*, that now sits beneath the Calton Hill at the east end of Princes Street, is recognised as his masterwork: a powerful Greek temple of block forms and solid doric columns.

In the building of these New Town monuments Hamilton's competitor was William Henry Playfair (1790–1857). Though not elected to the academy until 1829 Playfair was highly connected in Scotland's governing class, and a trained architect. It was Playfair who would complete some of the finest neo-classical buildings in Edinburgh and this would include The Royal Institution building at the foot of the Mound on Edinburgh's Princes Street, now the home of the Royal Scottish Academy. Playfair's diploma work was his *Design for the Surgeons' Hall*, from 1830, a building situated in the south-east of the city near his splendid Old College building for Edinburgh University.

Both architects had a fractious relationship with the academy, and indeed with each other. Playfair viewing Hamilton as a vulgar *arriviste* and Hamilton, in turn, recognised Playfair as an ill-disposed and intractable individual. At the birth of the Scottish Academy, however, these were key figures amongst the seven architects elected in the first years of the institution.

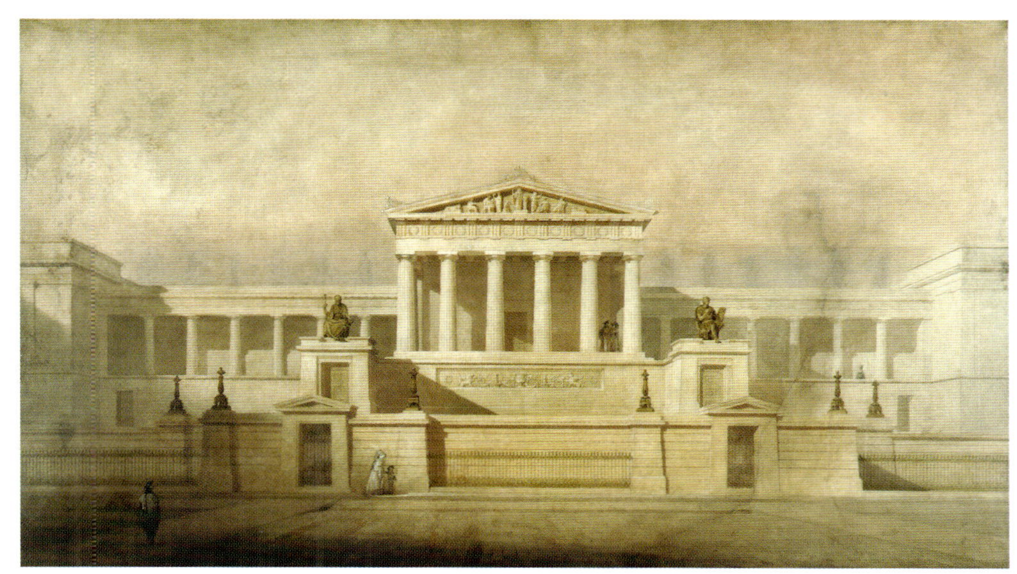

Thomas Hamilton, *Design for The Royal High School, Edinburgh, c.1825–31*

William Henry Playfair, *Design for Surgeons' Hall, Edinburgh, 1830–32*

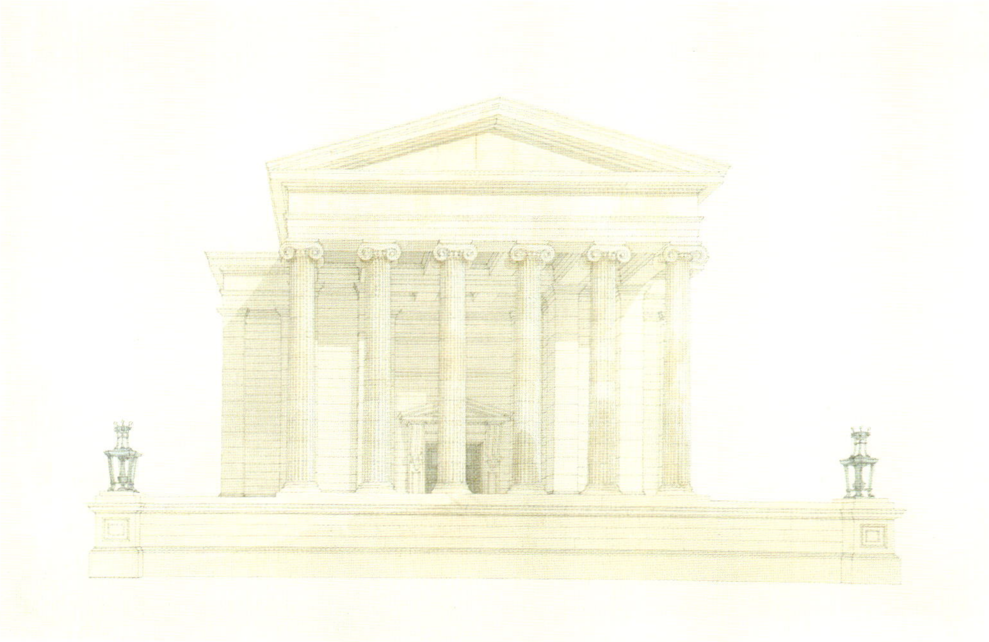

JOHN SYME, *The Solicitor General,*
Lord Cockburn

The building of Edinburgh's New Town was a marker that signalled an ambitious and modern sense of social development. Rooted in Enlightenment values it projected a rationalist and reformist vision of a revitalised capital city. These developments were tied to social change and particularly to a subtle class conflict that pitched an emergent bourgeoisie against a 'landed' and aristocratic elite. In some senses the embryonic Scottish Academy was representative of this emerging, professionalised and middle-class, alliance that re-orientated creative practice in a capitalist market-place.

The protagonists in this social change were celebrated individuals and were, naturally, recognised in the art of portraiture. John Syme (1795–1861) was distinguished as a portrait painter and had been a pupil of Henry Raeburn; indeed, as Raeburn's assistant he completed some of the master's work following Raeburn's sudden death in in 1834. Syme was a founder member of the Scottish Academy as was his uncle, Patrick Syme (1774–1845). Patrick, a notable painter of flowers and botanical images, was, in fact, to take the chair at the first meeting of the academy in May 1826. John Syme painted in a manner influenced by Raeburn but without the flair and colour of his tutor. In fact in 'The Scottish School of Painting' that sensitive reader of painting William Darling McKay (RSA 1883), himself a painter and an academician, notes that Syme painted in a manner 'more of the

Raeburn of an earlier time than of the period during which he had been associated with him. It looks as if the fuller qualities of the master's later years being beyond his reach, he had fallen back on the thinner, more mosaic-like manner of his first period' (McKay 127).

John Syme's diploma work is a portrait precisely in the manner that McKay described. *The Solicitor General, Lord Cockburn*, is dark in tone and lacking in the 'fuller' qualities of Raeburn. His subject, however, is a figure who exemplifies the tensions and changes of the age. Esteemed and connected, Cockburn was both an author of historical narratives – he was a significant commentator on the Disruption during 1843 – an advocate and a judge. From a privileged Tory background he became both a reformer and a Whig. A denizen of the New Town, with a house in Charlotte Square, he would become Lord Advocate of Scotland during the 1830s. Syme's portrait, then, reflects upon that class of individual who would shape the new Scotland and who exemplified the ambitions of the Scottish Academy: a reformist, sometimes conflicted, but generally 'modern' cast of mind that recognised the changing circumstances of the contemporary period.

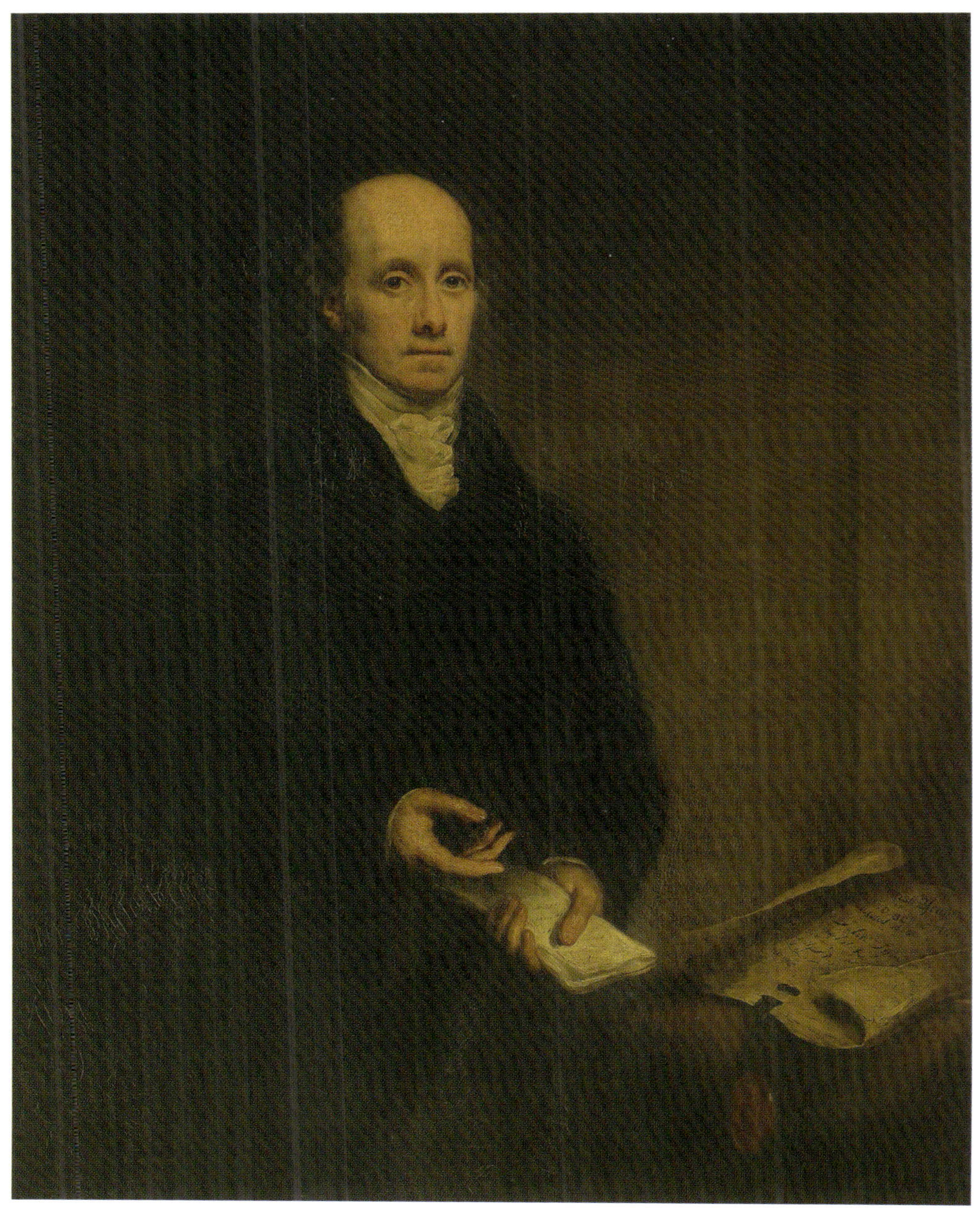

John Syme, *The Solicitor General, Lord Cockburn.*

PATRICK GIBSON, *Landscape Composition*

If architecture was responsible for the reshaping of Edinburgh's topography in the early nineteenth century and portraiture represented that class of people who would modernise Scotland's social, cultural and political world, then landscape painting was a companion star in this shifting galaxy. The genre of landscape matured in the 18th century and became a dimension of Scotland's art that reflected the sense of a varied and resonant geography replete with the echoes of history and circumstance. Landscape painting, of course, was subject to fluctuations in style and fashion and Scottish art is abundant in examples of classical, picturesque, panoramic and, especially, romantic views. But, at the founding of the Scottish Academy one of the principal styles was classical and this is the 'look' of Patrick Gibson's diploma submission.

A founder member of the Scottish Academy Patrick Gibson (c.1782–1829) had trained under Alexander Nasmyth – who no less a figure than David Wilkie would call 'the founder of the landscape painting of Scotland'. Later he would attend the Trustees Academy in Edinburgh, then under the stewardship of the influential painter and teacher John Graham. Nasmyth had been one of those ambitious Scottish artists who, in the late 18th century, would spend time studying in Rome and the inflection of Claude Lorrain would, for a period, inform his landscapes. On returning to Scotland Nasmyth would elide this classical and arcadian style with facets of a restrained picturesque aesthetic

and so create a unique sense of a confluent ideal and natural vision. This was generally informed, as Duncan Macmillan has noted in his seminal 'Painting in Scotland: the Golden Age', by a conception that is 'stable and harmonious' and incorporated a 'vision of human order within nature' (Macmillan 145).

Aspects of this lineage are evident in Gibson's *Landscape Composition*. He has created an imagined landscape centred upon a grove of gently twisting trees, framed by classical ruins, and recessing onto a stretch of water, a distant castle, and some highland hills. Under the trees, in the foreground, a figure is seen resting. Neither naturalistic nor romantic this work combines the manner of Claude lightly tempered by Nicolas Poussin and so creating a pastoral and arcadian idyll. These qualities are overlain with a muted sense of the picturesque to create a kind of dreamscape. Gibson was both a theorist of art and a harsh critic of his contemporaries but it might be said that his landscapes failed to echo the intellectual refinement or indeed the fundamental humanism of his great mentor Alexander Nasmyth. For all that *Landscape Composition* is characteristic of the momentum and direction of Scottish landscape painting at the birth of the Scottish Academy.

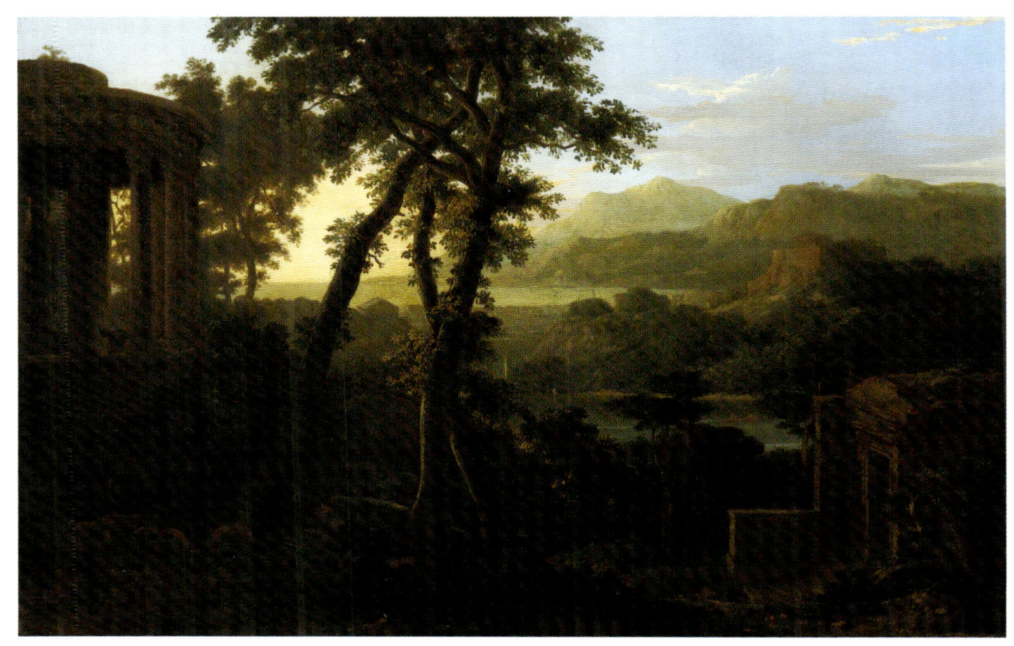

Patrick Gibson, *Landscape Composition*

JOHN STEELL, *David Scott* SA

Patrick Gibson had been one of the founding members of the academy but had previously been an active participant in the Associated Society of Artists and in the Royal Institution for the Encouragement of Fine Arts in Scotland; organisations that immediately preceded the establishment of the academy and were instrumental in its early history. This pattern of association was typical amongst artists who would become members of the academy in its early years and the sculptor John Steell (1804–1891) would exhibit both with the Royal Institution and with the Scottish Academy, accepting the role of elected academician in 1829 after the recognition of the academy as the dominant institution for Scotland's artists.

Steell was the most significant and esteemed Scottish sculptor of his generation, and indeed of the 19th century. In the year of his election to the academy he had studied in Rome, and following the success of his maquette for *Alexander and Bucephalous* no less a figure than Francis Chantrey encouraged him to set up his studio in London. That Steell chose to stay, and work, in Edinburgh was a testament to his commitment to a native sculpture. This commitment would see him model the archetypes of Scottish history and culture including the centrepiece of Edinburgh's Princes Street the marble statue of *Sir Walter Scott and his Dog* housed in the Scott Monument.

In some ways his work echoed the rational classicism of Edinburgh's New Town streetscape but there was a modern note to his sculpture for his figures were generally fashioned in contemporary dress and exhibited a subtle naturalism. His diploma work for the academy is a portrait bust of *David Scott* SA, and demonstrates his skill in modelling, carving and characterisation. His subject was his friend, the mercurial painter David Scott. Scott was known for his saturnine character and this was generally reflected in the subject matter of his art. Steell, however, has chosen to model the bust of Scott on the classical sculpture *The Dying Alexander* – discovered in Rome in the 16th century and now in the Uffizi Gallery in Florence. Here he presents the morose Scott as a youthful, tragic and idealistic figure: a melancholy visage topped by a tumult of waves and tendrils. Steell could move between a genre temperament, a monumental classicism and a formal naturalism in his work, but here he approaches a romanticism that befits the restless nature of his subject.

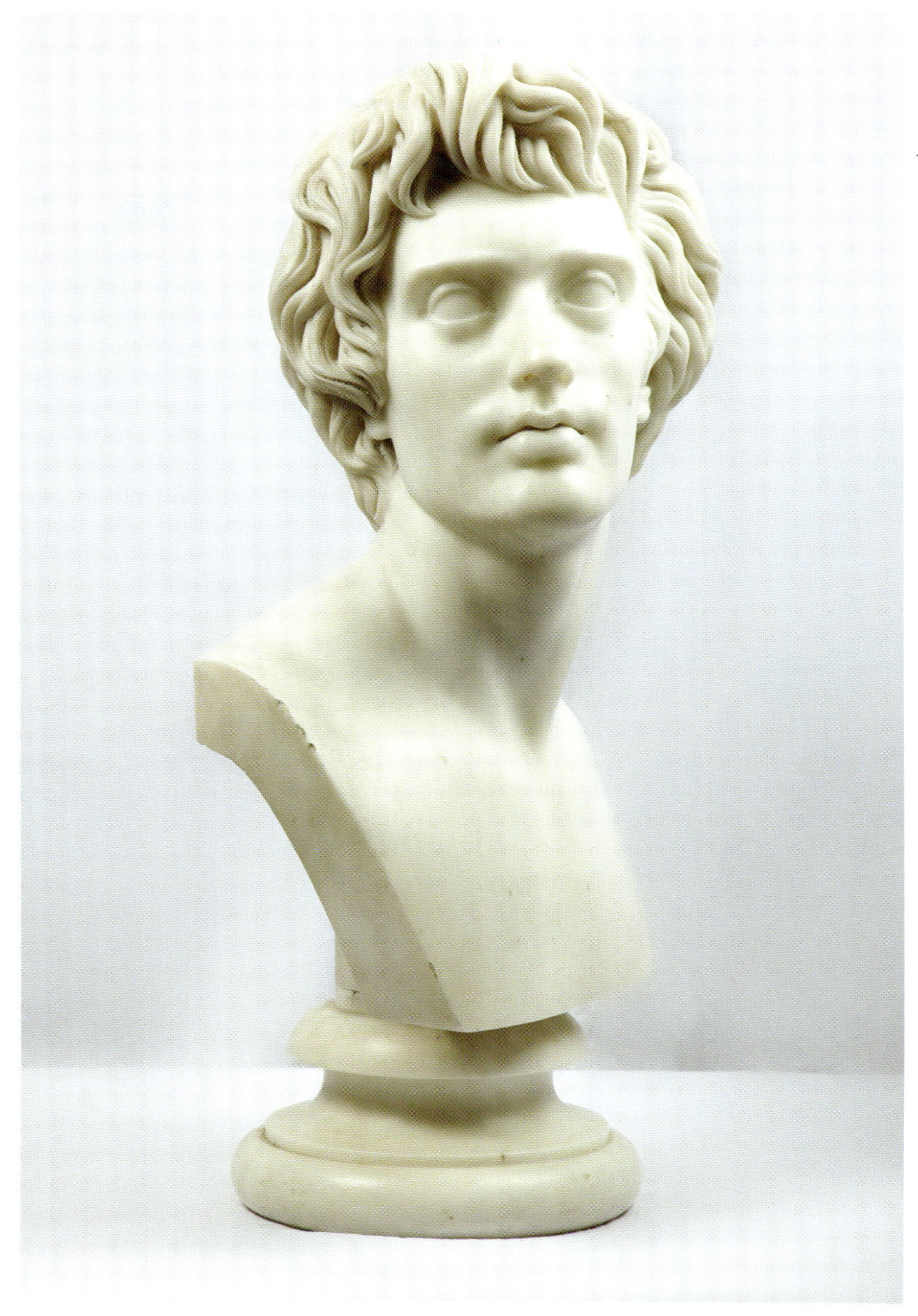

John Steell, *David Scott SA.*

DAVID SCOTT, *Cain Degraded (or Remorse)*

David Scott (1806–49) was, indeed, a remarkable and remarkably flawed artist. James Caw, in his seminal study 'Scottish Painting 1620–1908', published in 1908, suggests he 'was a born painter, but fate denied him that early training without which the most splendid natural gifts are crippled and can hardly attain fruition'. He would add that 'Scott's art is worthy of praise and high admiration' (Caw, 124) but these mixed reviews are typical of the reception given to this troubled painter and poet.

Elected to the academy in 1829 his training as an artist was, indeed, fractured. His father, Robert Scott, was an engraver and apprenticed the young David in the craft. Despite the financial imperatives occasioned by family needs he was allowed some training in the Trustees Academy and, in 1827, became a founder member of the Edinburgh Life Academy Association, so practicing drawing from the model. His temperament fed into his taste in art and subjects like *The Hopes of Early Genius dispelled by Death*, 1828, *The Dead Sarpedon borne by Sleep and Death*, c.1831, and the drawing *Burying the Dead*, c.1831, spoke to his dark and morose character. Even his stay in Italy, during 1832–3, saw him critique and reject the formal qualities of the Old Masters. Generally his work was large in scale, dramatic in atmosphere and ran counter to the tastes of the period. Following his early death his reputation was saved through the memoir written by his brother, the successful Pre-Raphaelite painter William Bell Scott (HRSA 1887), and by the positive commentary from W. B. Scott's close friend Dante Gabriel Rossetti.

Cain Degraded is an extraordinary work and typical of David Scott's oeuvre. Large in scale and dramatic in content, it is a dark, near monochrome, vision of alienation and despair. In a raw, mountainous landscape, the near-naked outcast covers his ears in order to block-out the taunts of his tormentors. On his forehead the 'mark of Cain' is writ large. Scott had a fascination with religious imagery, but this is typical in the choice of a subject that describes an arc across betrayal, death, suffering, humiliation and rejection. The visceral and abstract qualities of the image being a parallel to the artist's morose disposition.

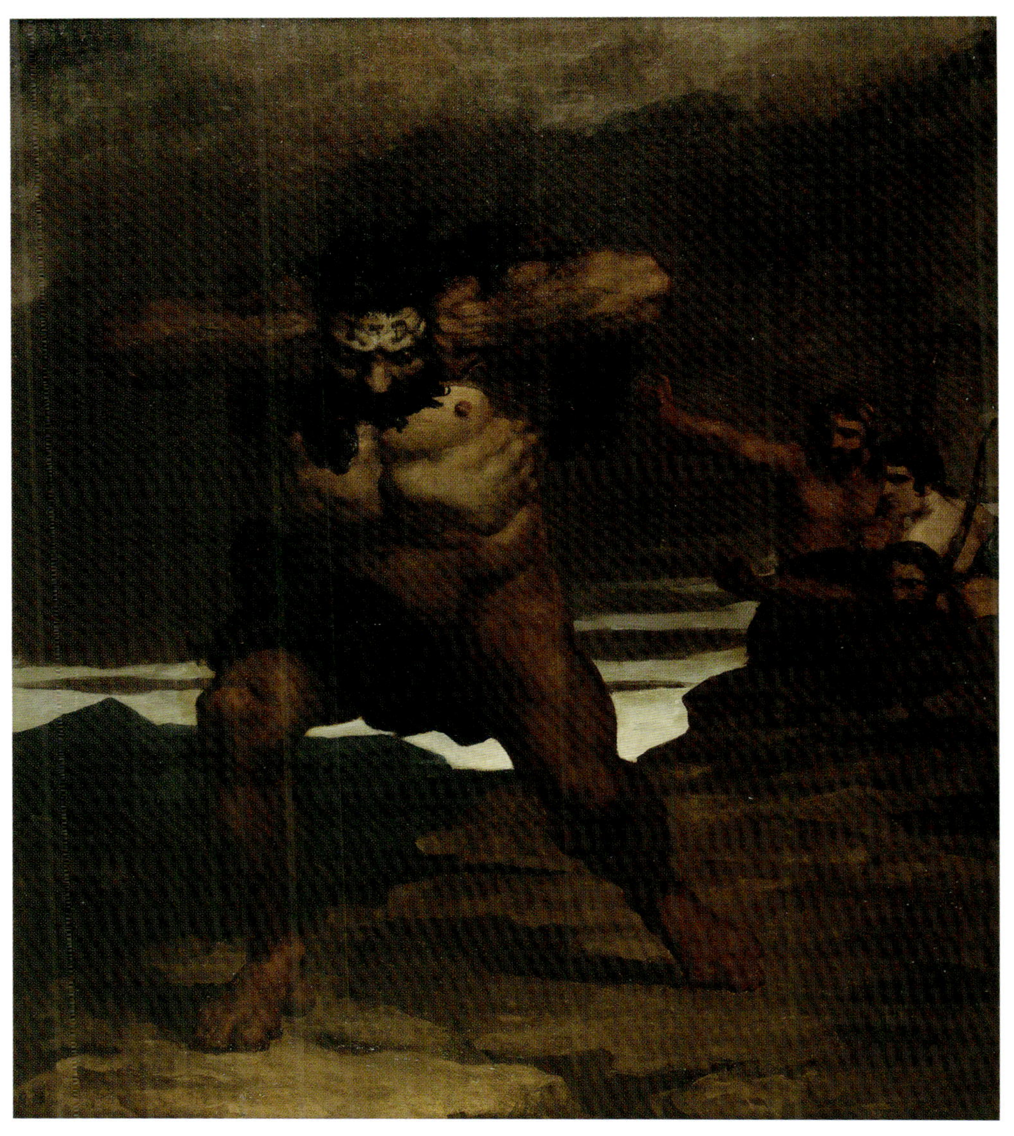

David Scott, *Cain Degraded (or Remorse)*

JAMES GILES, *The Weird Wife o' Lang Stane Lea*

Religious themes and paintings were a staple of academic art in the 19th century and this was certainly the case in Scotland. David Scott had selected an Old Testament subject and dramatised it in his inimitable style. More traditional subjects in a more orthodox style were available as diploma submissions with, for example, John A. P. Houston (RSA 1845) *The Good Samaritan;* James Eckford Lauder (RSA 1846) *Hagar* and, William Hole (RSA 1889) *If Thou Had'st Known.*

In Presbyterian Scotland, however, the demonic was ever present as an inevitable counterpoint to the divine. James Giles (1801–70) was a landscape painter of some note. Working from Aberdeen he came under the patronage of the Earl of Aberdeen who commissioned, from Giles, a panoply of images depicting Scottish castles. He may also have been instrumental in securing commissions from Queen Victoria. After 1852 Victoria's summer residence was at the Balmoral estate on Deeside and she encouraged artists to complete landscape, and even portrait, images relating to the estate. Giles, who had travelled in Europe and been resident in Rome during 1824–5, was a consummate landscape painter, often in an Italianate manner, and was favoured by Royal patronage at Balmoral.

However, elected to the Scottish Academy in 1829, Giles submitted, as his diploma work, one of the strangest and most esoteric paintings in the collection. *The Weird Wife o' Lang Stane Lea* depicts a gloaming scene in a wild landscape. A group of standing stones is lit by a crescent moon that arcs around a single star. Striding through this scene is a figure wrapped in a cowl and carrying a stick. The 'weird wife' has her back to the viewer and seems intent on some mission. In the foreground, to the right of the image, there is a hare. This is an imagined landscape and an uncanny scene. It may connote the mysterious standing stone circles that pepper the county, the 'lang stane lea' may relate to sites on the outskirts of Aberdeen including areas where witch trials occurred, and the hare may be presented as a witch's 'familiar'. Certainly Giles has run counter to the measured and conventional landscapes of which he was an acknowledged master and has presented to the academy a cryptic and even a sinister image.

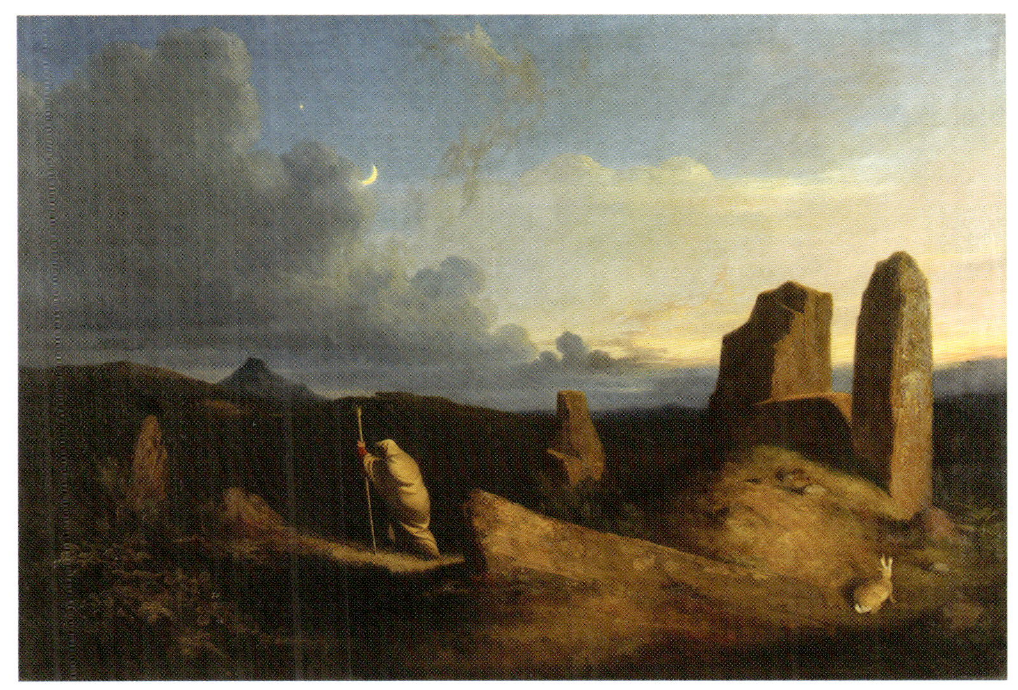

James Giles, *The Weird Wife o' Lang Stane Lea*

WILLIAM BORTHWICK JOHNSTONE, *Scene at Holyrood 1566*

For all the strangeness of James Giles' diploma work it is a truth that amongst this first generation of academicians subject matter was determined by the fashions of the period. Here, the commonplace subjects would be historical scenes and genre paintings. The founding of the Scottish Academy, in 1826, occurred only four years after George IV's visit to Edinburgh: an event choreographed by Sir Walter Scott and replete with the insignia of Scottish identity. John Morrison, in 'Painting the Nation', has emphasized the 'Highlandism' of this festival for Scott ensured that Edinburgh was 'bedecked with tartan and awash with Highlanders' (Morrison 48). But the issue of Scottish identity reached beyond this conception to episodes in Scottish history that chimed with a muted nationalism.

William Borthwick Johnstone (1804–68) provided, as his diploma piece, a painting titled *Scene at Holyrood 1566*. Johnstone came late to painting for his training was the law, and indeed he practiced as a lawyer. Having taken evening classes in art at the Trustees Academy he began to exhibit at the Scottish Academy from 1836, becoming a full academician only in 1848. In history painting, and especially in genre, the dominant figure of the period was David Wilkie and Johnstone is known to have admired his work. Indeed he became a friend of most significant artists of the period and was a protagonist in art world politics of the period, he was also invaluable to the academy as Treasurer and as Librarian during the 1850s.

Scene at Holyrood 1566 is a set piece historical drama that would be resonant for the academy's audience when exhibited in 1855. The cult of Mary, Queen of Scots, still flourished during the Victorian period and was a *leitmotif* of European art and culture. Johnstone has chosen the murder of David Rizzio as his subject. During the turbulent years of Mary's rule the internecine struggles of the Scottish nobility, fractured, also, by religious turmoil and the ambitions of Elizabeth I from south of the border, ensured every level of dramatic tragedy. Mary, in 1566 married to Darnley, but under suspicion of having been made pregnant by her secretary, the Italian and catholic David Rizzio, was under siege from enemies on all sides. In a planned assassination led by Lord Ruthven her private chambers at the Palace of Holyrood were invaded and Rizzio murdered before her eyes. Johnstone creates a tableaux of the aftermath with the body of Rizzio surrounded by his assassins while the distraught Queen is attended behind an arras. The theatre and drama of the painting is designed to conjure with history and identity in all of its convoluted formations.

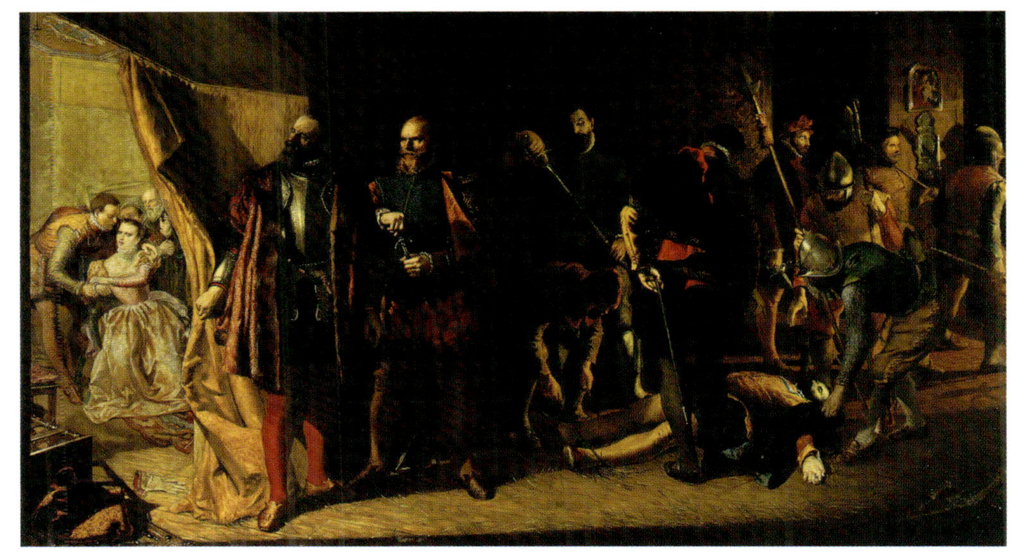

William Borthwick Johnstone, *Scene at Holyrood 1566*

CHARLES LEES, *The Summer Moon*
– Bait Gatherers

History painting would certainly be a common trope in academy exhibitions for it recognized the different traditions and circumstances of the Scottish nation. Typical amongst these would be images of Jacobite rebellion like John Blake MacDonald's (RSA 1877) image of massacre titled *Glencoe, 1692* and, George Ogilvy Reid's (RSA 1898) painting *After Killiecrankie.* But David Wilkie had become one of the most significant international artists of his generation following the success of his genre painting *Pitlessie Fair* in 1805, and he helped establish a taste for genre that ran deep into the 19th century.

In an era of industrialization, and in a sophisticated European city like Edinburgh, it is something of a paradox that the walls of the academy might be strewn with images of rural activity and peasant life. But the taste for a nostalgic and more 'organic' human society ran deep in the rapidly changing social scene of Victorian capitalism. Charles Lees (1800–1880) would become renown as a painter of sporting scenes, and he specialised in episodes from the world of golf and curling. He was also a recognised portrait painter having trained, as a young man, under Raeburn. Completing his artistic education he travelled to Rome in 1832: though this followed a colourful interlude in London where he eloped (to marry in Gretna Green) with the daughter of dignitary.

However, following his election as an academician in 1830 his diploma submission was neither portrait painting, sporting image, nor Roman landscape, for it was a fashionable genre piece. Lees chose to submit a moonlit scene by the seashore. When genre painters did not paint bucolic peasants in episodes of rustic theatre they invariably travelled to the fringes of Scotland where fisherfolk engaged their unique way of life. Lees' *The Summer Moon – Bait Gatherers* is a romantic view of women and children digging for bait on the seashore. The tide is low on the foreshore, the sea calm, and the twilight scene bathed by a golden glow from the soft, summer moon. Out at sea tall, rigged sailing ships lie anchored accompanied by smaller boats and sailing luggers. In the foreground a single wave laps the seashore. This is a painting of littoral life created as a counterpoint to the industry and activity of the urban world. Displayed at the academy building in Edinburgh it would speak to ideas of harmony and content in a period of transformation and fracture.

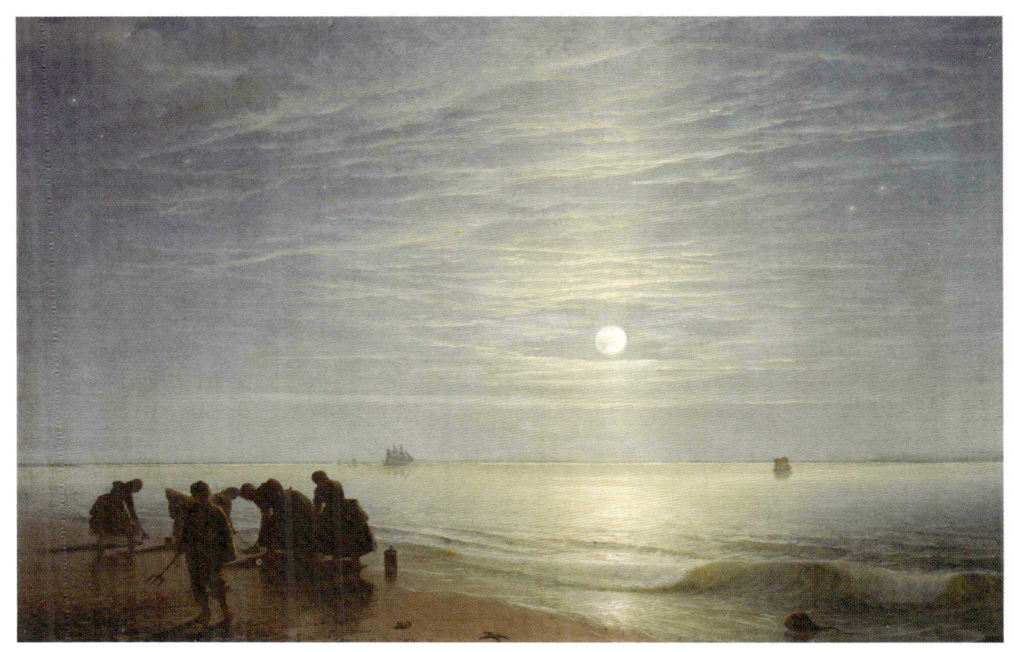

Charles Lees, *The Summer Moon – Bait Gatherers*

JOSEPH NOEL PATON, *Oberon and Titania – first study for The Quarrel*

Charles Lees' painting of fisherfolk was a commonplace subject by the 1850s. In fact it had been popularised in Scotland, and in the academy, by the pioneering photographic works of David Octavius Hill and Robert Adamson. The partnership's photographs of the Newhaven fishing community were taken between 1843 and 1847, and have become keystones in the photographic canon. Hill (RSA 1830), a prominent landscape painter, was an esteemed Secretary to the Scottish Academy almost from its inception and up until his death in 1870. He had a friendship with the artist Joseph Noel Paton (1821–1901), and they were related by marriage; for Hill's second wife was the eminent Victorian sculptor Amelia Robertson Paton, sister to Joseph Noel.

The Patons were a distinguished artistic family hailing from Dunfermline, in Fife, where their father Joseph Neil Paton was a prominent designer in Dunfermline's damask linen industry. Three of Joseph Neil's children became artists, and two of them academicians. Amelia, though highly respected and the recipient of many public commissions was probably excluded, in this period, on grounds of gender. The youngest son, Waller Hugh Paton, was an associate of the Pre-Raphaelites and elected an academician in 1865 when he provided a characteristic landscape painting *Lamlash Bay – Isle of Arran* as his diploma work. Joseph Noel Paton, one year younger than Amelia, was elected to the academy in 1850.

Joseph Noel Paton's election was merited for he was a significant figure not only in Scottish but in British art. From 1843 a friend of John Everett Millais his painting was influenced by the tenor of the Pre-Raphaelites throughout the 1850s. In the Victorian fashion he became best known for detailed narrative studies often based on literary sources. His signature works remain the extraordinary paintings *The Reconciliation of Oberon and Titania*, of 1847, and *The Quarrel of Oberon and Titania*, from 1849. Though based on fanciful episodes in Shakespeare's 'A Midsummer Night's Dream' these are classic Victorian 'fairy' paintings: they explored issues of fantasy, imagination, and a discreet surrogate eroticism. For his diploma work Paton submitted a study for *Oberon and Titania*, though the academy would purchase his *The Reconciliation of Oberon and Titania* soon after its completion in 1847 – this was subsequently transferred to the National Gallery of Scotland in 1910. Typical of Paton it is an incredibly detailed work, full of incident and diversion, and rewarding the minutest investigation. For, in a magical fairy glade, he presents a riot of pixies, brownies, sprites and woodland animals circling the quarrelling lovers.

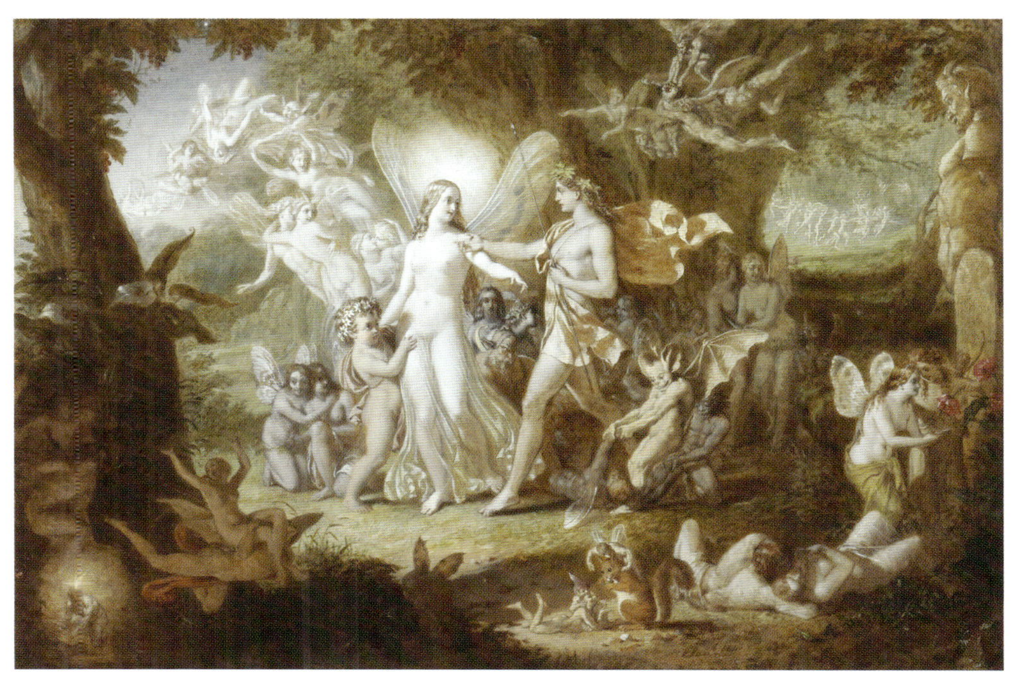

Joseph Noel Paton, *Oberon and Titania – first study for The Quarrel*

SAMUEL BOUGH, *Edinburgh from Bonnington*

This first generation of academicians had been elected into a Scottish Academy and this was an institution in contest with competing professional organisation. By the time Joseph Noel Paton was elected it was to the Royal Scottish Academy, for the academy had been awarded its Royal Charter in 1838. In consequence the academy was recognised as *the* institution representing professional artists in Scotland and was henceforth regarded as something of an 'establishment'.

Samuel Bough (1822–1878) was elected an academician in 1875 though he had been made an associate member, ARSA, in 1856. His acceptance to full membership was long delayed largely because of difficult relationships with some established members. Bough's training as an artist had been rudimentary. As a young man he worked with an engraving firm in London; he became a theatre scene painter in Manchester, and attended some life classes at the local academy; by 1849 he was a scene painter in Glasgow, subsequently painting landscapes in the environs of Cadzow Forest; and, by 1855, he was resident in Edinburgh submitting landscapes and marine paintings to the academy exhibitions. Originally a native of Carlisle he painted throughout Europe and particularly on the coast of Fife, but he remained resident in Edinburgh until his death. His landscapes and marine painting were generally sketched *en plein air* and finished in the studio, and his

work was largely inflected by the example of Turner.

There is, indeed, a hint of Turner in Bough's diploma submission of 1875. *Edinburgh from Bonnington* is a landscape that looks from the north of the city southwards towards the castle high on its rock. The foreground is largely rural with the Water of Leith meandering past a farmyard and with farmhands working in the fields. In the distance the smoke and industry of 'Auld Reekie' is all too evident though flecked in shades of blue under a broken sky, threatening a shower of rain. Bonnington was, originally, a small village on the outskirts of Edinburgh though by Bough's time it was part of a thoroughfare from the city to the port of Leith, in fact adjacent to Leith Walk. Bough has, evidently, positioned himself in a secluded and semi-rural area but the sense of change and modernity remains a discreet element in the painting. In the middle-ground, and to the left of the painting, a trail of smoke announced the progress of a steam train. It would be too much to associate this painting with Turner's epic *Rain, Steam and Speed – the Great Western Railway*, of 1844, but a memory of this masterpiece may well have been to mind for Bough. His painting, by contrast, is a modest and charming landscape redolent of change in his adopted city.

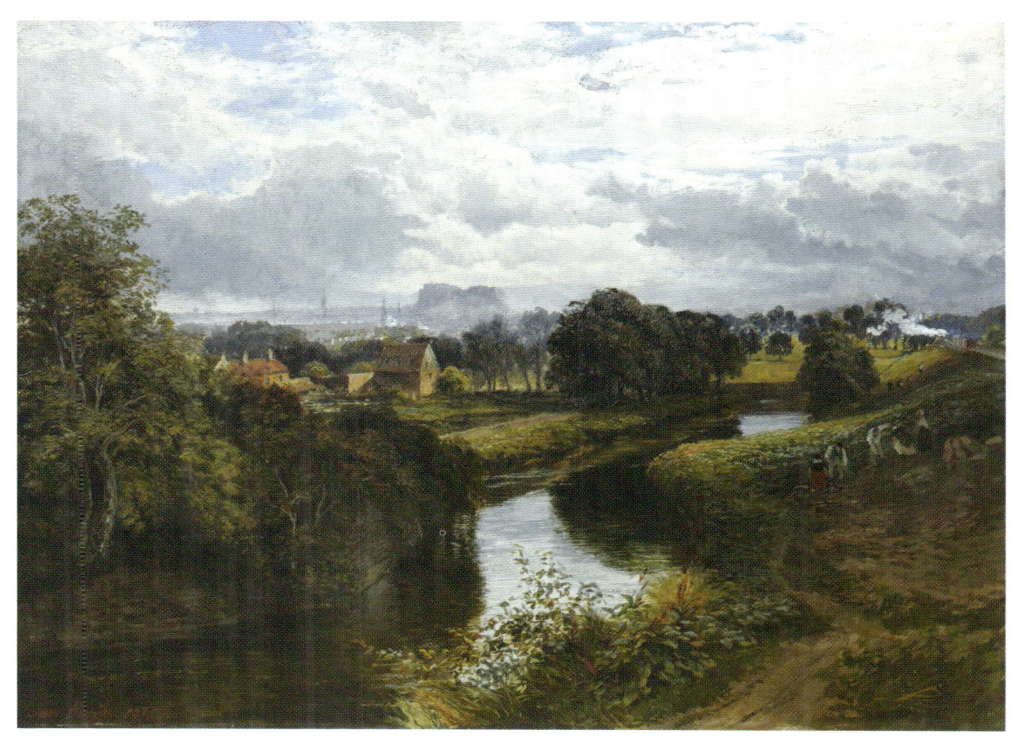

Samuel Bough, *Edinburgh from Bonnington*

WILLIAM FLEMING VALLANCE,
Reading the War News

Samuel Bough was born in England but made his profession in Scotland, becoming a member of the Royal Scottish Academy. Many Scottish artists, Joseph Noel Paton being an example, were equally at home in the Royal Academy in London as they were in the Edinburgh institution. In many ways these associations spoke to the sometimes benign, sometimes fretted, relationship between 'Britishness' and 'Scottishness' in the second half of the 19th century.

However, it might be argued that George IV's visit to Edinburgh, with all it's *faux* Scottish pageantry, was possible because the idea of being Scottish and being British was no longer a contested identity at this time; in fact, that the shadow of 'the '45' was no longer fearsome. In this sense William Fleming Vallance's *Reading the War News* spoke to a settled sense of Britishness in which the notion of being, also, Scottish was not problematic.

Vallance (1827–1904) had a fractured early life having worked first as a weaver and then as a gilder to the esteemed Edinburgh dealers in art Aitken Dott. It was the early 1850s before he received any formal training in drawing, but, by 1855, he was under the tutelage of Robert Scott Lauder (RSA 1829). Lauder taught at the Trustees Academy in Edinburgh and produced a golden generation of artists who broke with Victorian conventions in art to produce freely painted, high key, images. James Caw, in his landmark early history of Scottish art *Scottish Painting 1620–1908*,

noted that Vallance 'had been brought up in Leith, and it was as a painter of the sea and seafaring life to which he turned his attention as early as 1860' and added 'he expressed with considerable dexterity… much of the charm of silvery light playing over delicate grey-green surges, or of sunshine filtering through summer haze upon calm waters busy with shipping' (Caw 263).

Vallance was elected to the academy in 1881 and his diploma work *Reading the War News* was completed in that year. This seascape depicts moored boats peopled by seamen frantically reading a newspaper for news of the war. In 1881 the significant British involvement in war was in the First Boer War, and it may be that this image relates to that conflict. Significantly, however, Vallance was reprising a theme from one of the most successful paintings of the 19th century, David Wilkie's *The Chelsea Pensioners Reading the Waterloo Dispatch*, of 1822. Here Scottish and British regiments had been engaged in international conflict and the sense of 'Union' was material.

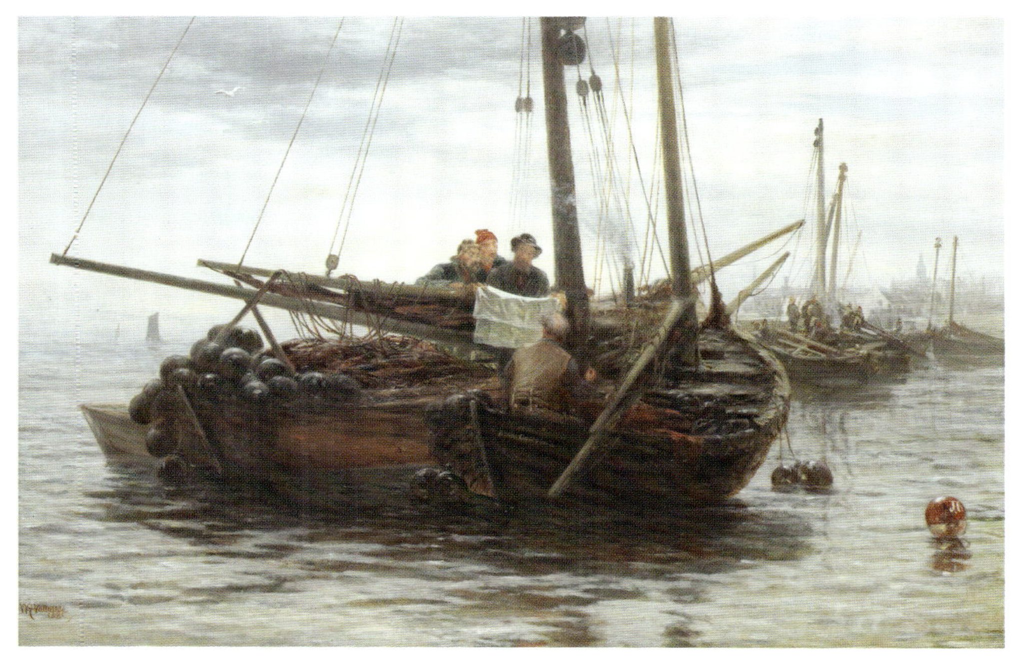

William Fleming Vallance, *Reading the War News*

ROBERT GIBB, *The Sea King*

The archetypal painter of British military action, in the 19th century, was a Scot who became celebrated for his paintings of battle scenes and of Scottish regiments in conflict; this was Robert Gibb (1845–1932). From 1878 Gibb painted chiefly military scenes and some portraits, but his reputation and career was established by his famed painting *The Thin Red Line*, from 1881. This painting was based on the actions of the 93rd Highland Regiment at Balaklava in the Crimea during 1854, but the element of research and attention to detail in the work was typical of Gibb's approach. Subsequent works explored aspects of the Napoleonic Wars, the Indian Rebellion, and even the First World War, but in the majority of instances Gibb focused upon the actions of Scottish regiments and displayed their tartanry, and heroism, in meticulous detail.

Gibb was a clear example of a 19th-century Scottish artist who had accepted the idea of 'Britishness' but who nevertheless reflected upon the theme of a distinctive Scottish identity. Prior to his becoming a painter of military scenes – and the King's Limner in Scotland from 1908 – he had explored the subject of northern history and culture. Amongst his earliest works there was *Columba in Sight of Iona*, from 1874, and *The Death of Columba*, from 1876. These images, it can be argued, signalled a concern with the particularity of Scottish identity expressed as a bonding and melding of clannish characteristics. Equally, his *The Last Voyage of the Viking* and *The Sea King*, both from 1883, presented a view of northern blending through the ravages of historical conflict.

In fact these early works were romantic in tone, and perhaps touched by a nascent symbolism. They offered a fantasy creation myth for Scotland that intersected clan and tribal loyalties with early Christian history and the trauma of sporadic invasion accompanied by inclusive settlement. They were also profoundly masculine in their manner, presenting the heroic male as the arbiter of human life and civilisation. Following his election to the academy in 1882 Gibb's diploma work was, in fact, *The Sea King* and it can be suggested that this presentation, created two years after the painting of *The Thin Red Line*, was calculated to foreground the notion of northern identity for the northern academy. Every inch the Viking, perhaps even Celtic, warrior the Sea King rests on his bearskin rug looking out to sea. A chainmail tunic, a spear, a golden earring and wristbands, and with his cloak pinned by a decorated brooch he is the perfect fabrication of the adventurer and warrior; and so, also, a profoundly Victorian icon of masculinity. But the discrete content of this image may yet be the presence of an underlying Scottish identity that conflicts with the dominant model of the 'British' hero.

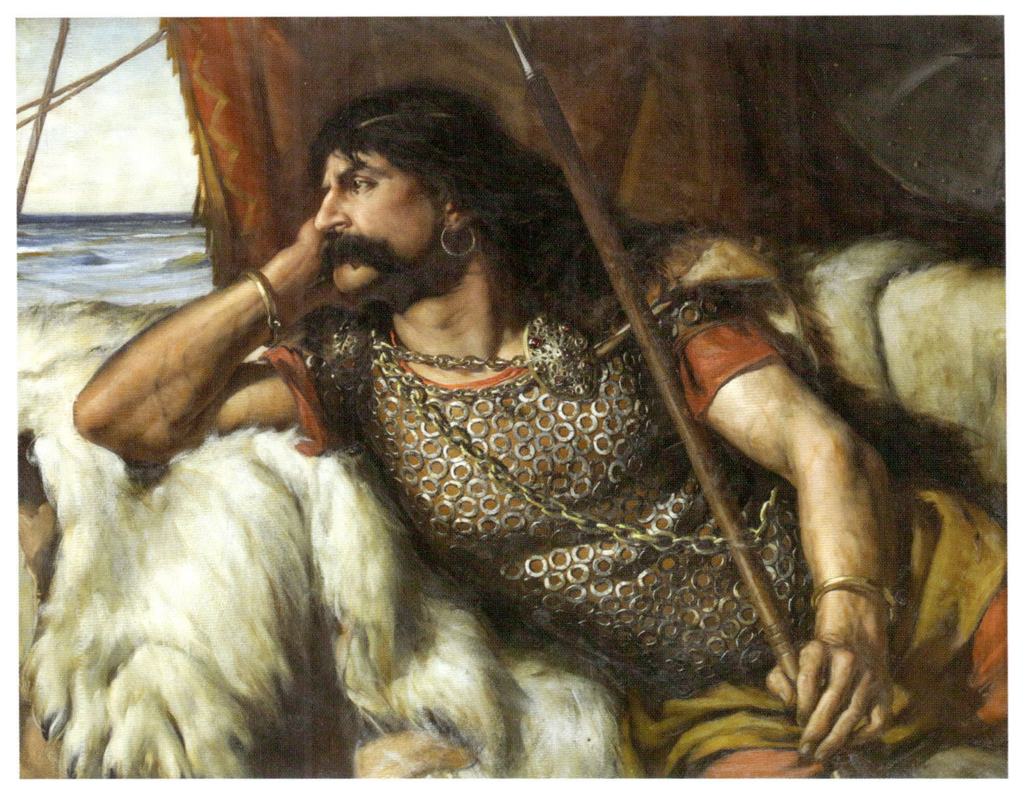

Robert Gibb, *The Sea King*

WILLIAM BEATTIE BROWN, *Coire-na-Faireamh, in Applecross Deer Forest, Ross-shire*

Issues of history and identity were a common feature of Scottish art, even if this was not framed as an overt 'nationalism'. These would emerge in every aspect of academic art from portraits that referenced significant figures in politics and culture, to history painting that focused upon significant moments in Scotland's story, to genre and its fascination with the vernacular and the everyday lives of Scotland's people, and to the quasi-Celtic symbolism of much romantic painting. Landscape painting, however, was not only one of the most familiar forms to those who would visit the academy but was loaded with association, memory and myth and so was replete with meaning for the academy's audience.

William Beattie Brown's (1831–1909) *Coire-na-Faireamh* is an epic of its type. Painted in 1883 it was submitted as his diploma work following his election as academician in 1884. A darkly romantic, brooding and intense study of the Highland wilderness it conjures every level of thought and association. Brown began to exhibit in the academy in his mid-30s and subsequently would also show in the Royal Academy in London. His landscape painting would be popular in both institutions for it spoke to the idea of an untamed wilderness just beyond the pale of the modern, urban and industrial society that was the dominant character of Victorian Britain. Certainly it was this conceit that had been popularized by an artist like Edwin Landseer and that was favoured by royal patronage.

Coire-na-Faireamh, however, spoke to associations beyond the romance of 'wilderness'. The high peaks of the distant hills tower over a glistening loch, the foreground moor of heather and rough grass is speckled with rocks and casual water, and in the mid-ground a solitary deer. *Coire-na-Faireamh* presents a landscape in the Applecross peninsula, in the far north-west of Scotland and a gateway to the Isle of Skye. Historically this was an area deeply affected by the Highland 'Clearances' and the depopulation of the area has been a matter of painful record. Brown's landscape, certainly in the 19th century, would have projected this association and so it represented remembered history, and the tragic experience of the Highland population. Certainly it also suggested notions of geological time, of the fractured ice-formed pre-history of the landscape; and even thoughts of nature as the untameable 'beyond'; but, the solitary deer in this evocative work stood for the clearance of a local Gaelic population that was to be replaced by the commercial 'crops' of sheep and deer.

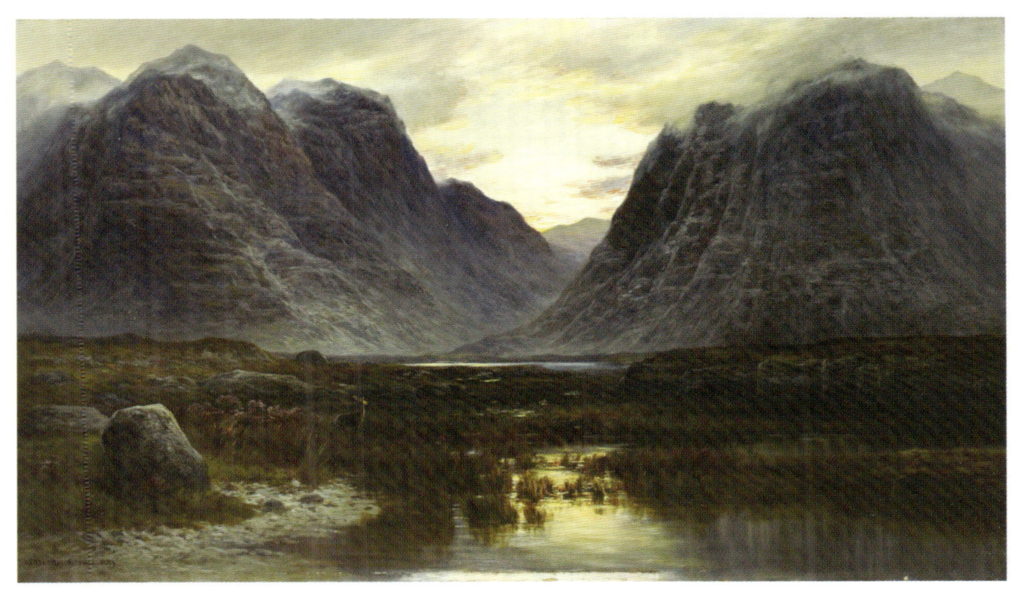

William Beattie Brown, *Coire-na-Faireamh, in Applecross Deer Forest, Ross-shire*

JAMES PITTENDRIGH MACGILLIVRAY,
The Right Reverend Monsignor Munro

Whereas nationalism was a discrete part of most academic art in this period it was an overt aspect of James Pittendrigh Macgillivray's fulsome character and personality. Macgillivray (1856–1938) was, effectively, the heir to John Steell's mantle as the eminent Scottish sculptor of his generation and the public memorialist of Scotland's society.

A true renaissance man – he was painter, poet, musician, cultural theorist, public commentator, and *provocateur*, as well as sculptor – he helped shape the social and cultural landscape of his time. Following a strenuous apprenticeship with the sculptor William Brodie he moved to Glasgow where he became an associate of 'The Glasgow Boys' and worked with Charles Rennie Mackintosh. He returned to Edinburgh in 1890, and like Steell viewed it as a matter of political and cultural import to remain, and to work, in Scotland. His first large scale public commission was for the statue of *Robert Burns* in Irvine from 1893, and throughout that decade he would attain success as the pre-eminent sculptor in Scotland.

Ever the controversialist he nevertheless was elected an academician in 1901; though he had previously attacked the academy in his poem 'Anent a Scots Academy', and had been a thorn in the side of the National Galleries of Scotland and even the education system for Scottish artists. However, his public works remained vigorous and he was prized for his studies of the portrait bust. John Tonge, in his polemical, and nationalist, 'The Arts of Scotland' noted that '(Macgillivray's) highly individualized bronze portraits are more powerfully modelled than any of his English contemporaries', and added that 'Artistically, his most satisfactory works are those in which the concern with facial expression finds an outlet in undisguised portraiture, in which the immediacy of the characterization is matched by spontaneity of handling' (Tonge 112–3). Certainly Macgillivray's portrait busts were much influenced by Rodin: and he paid a special attention to facture, the sculptor's expressive mark, and the relationship of the head to the base and pedestal. For all this his diploma submission, a portrait of the senior catholic clergyman Alexander Munro, was a work from c.1892 and though a powerful and serious study it predates the influence of Rodin. And so the head is smoothly modelled and given a clear and ascetic presence. Macgillivray remains, however, one of the academy's most ebullient characters at the turn of the 20th century.

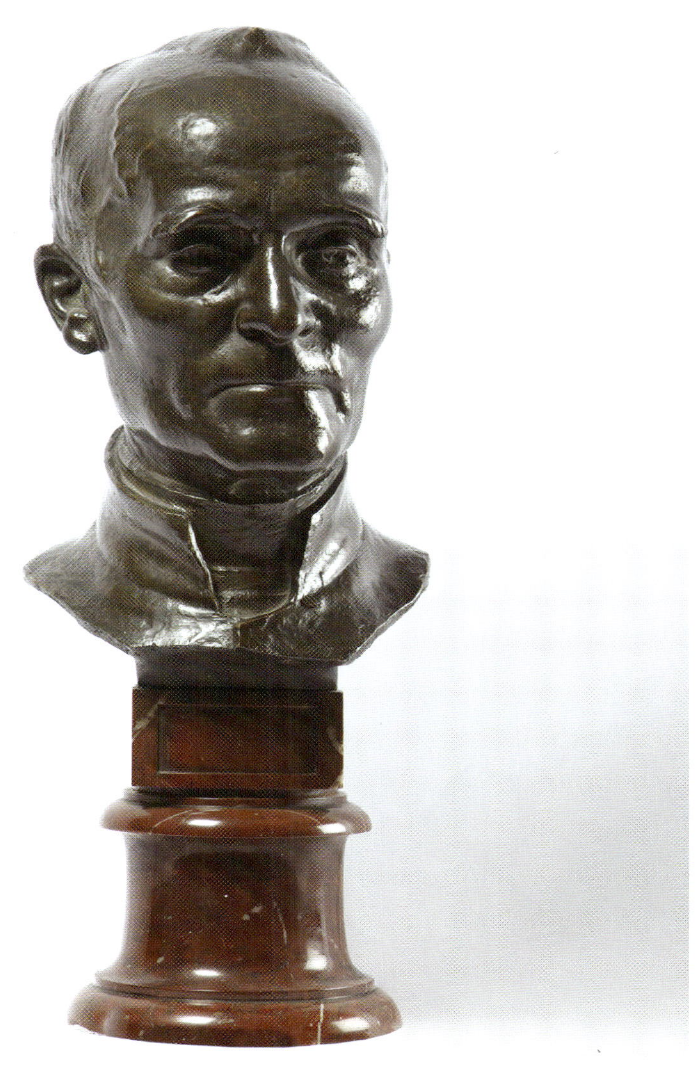

James Pittendrigh Macgillivray, *The Right Reverend Monsignor Munro*

ROBERT MCGREGOR, *Man goeth forth to his work and to his labour until evening*

ROBERT ALEXANDER, *Wat and Wearie*

JOSEPH DENOVAN ADAM, *Evening, Strathspey (or The Glory of Dying Day)*

Towards the close of the 19th century the most popular and so the most typical representations dressing the walls of the academy would be genre paintings; a taste established by David Wilkie at the very start of the century. Genre, itself, had been subject to changing fashion, most especially in continental Europe where visions of peasant life had been inflected with a political realism that radicalized the style. An element of this may been seen on Robert McGregor's (1847–1922) diploma work *Man goeth forth to his work and to his labour until evening*, a painting completed in the year before his election as academician in 1889. Certainly the painting has a religious tone, and it praises the virtue of hard work, but an echo of Millet can be seen here and perhaps even a note of the revolutionary Courbet.

The more conventional, and sentimental, tone of genre painting is evidenced in the painting of Robert Alexander (1840–1923) and especially in his diploma work *Wat and Wearie*. Elected to the academy in 1888 Alexander made a professional living by painting dogs and sometimes horses for the 'country' market. These works could be cloying and mawkish and might be regarded as the common fare of an unambitious painter. His diploma work has the merit of an association with the conditions of rural labour in a desperate contest with nature, and with a freedom of execution that demonstrates a genuine facility with paint.

Of course the market for animal paintings was nearly as profitable as that for genre and Joseph Denovan Adam (1842–1896) built his career on these images usually within a Highland setting. Elected to the academy in 1892, Adam submitted his *Evening, Strathspey* as his diploma presentation. The painting is remarkable for is combination of a traditional rural scene, complete with Adam's trademark cattle, and a twilight setting that affords a near impressionist concern with the play of light on landscape. By the 1890s this sense of an 'impressionist' technique would be familiar in Europe, and in Scotland, but would be less commonplace within the academy. In some degree Adam's work, one of his most ambitious, signalled the changes that were to come.

Robert McGregor, *Man goeth forth to his work and to his labour until evening*

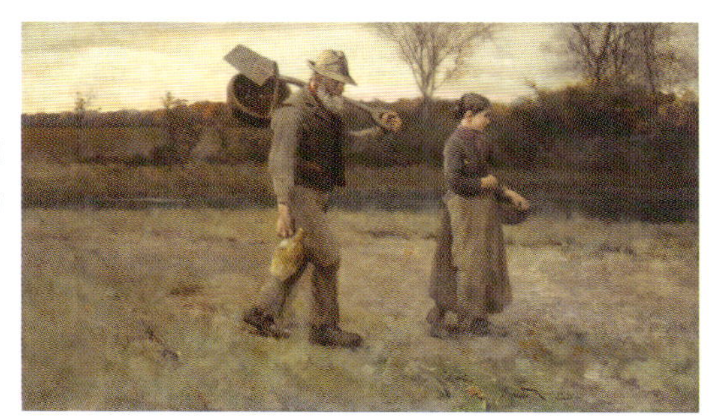

Robert Alexander, *Wat and Wearie*

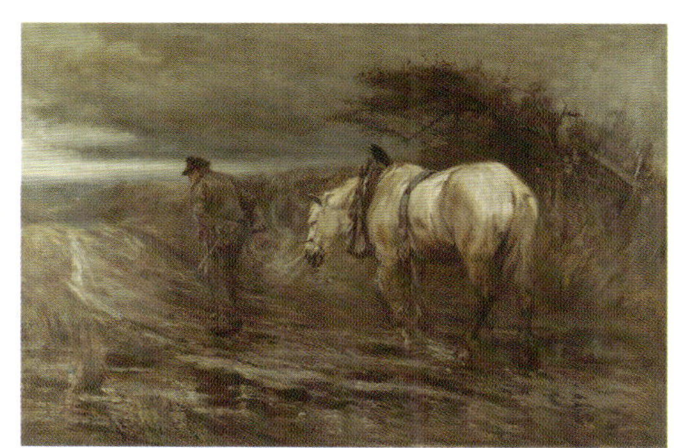

Joseph Denovan Adam, *Evening, Strathspey (or The Glory of Dying Day)*

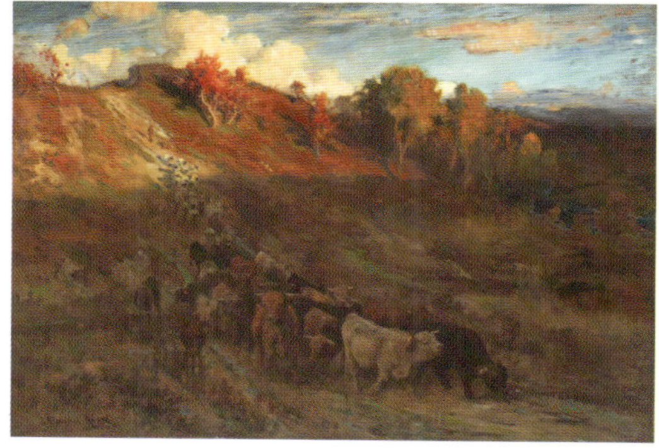

The generation of artists who came to prominence in the 1880s and 1890s began to reject the conventions of Victorian art and reached out towards a nuanced modernism. Some evidence of this may be seen in Adam's high-keyed painting of *Evening, Strathspey* but a richer and fuller sense of modern art was evidenced in diploma submissions at the close of the 19th and the opening of the 20th century.

Robert Lorimer (1864–1929) was not elected a full member of the academy until 1921 but he chose as his diploma work a landmark architectural project from the period c.1892. Lorimer's career as an architect began in the offices of Rowan Anderson – the designer of the Scottish National Portrait Gallery – and he honed his skills in architectural practice in London before returning to Edinburgh. His first significant commission following this return was the restoration of Earlshall in Fife, and the design for this seminal scheme became his diploma work. Lorimer based his subtle restoration of the 16th-century building and the magnificent gardens upon the earlier restoration of Kellie Castle in Fife, a family home that had been sensitively restored by his father, James Lorimer. His model for the restoration, however, was the blending of vernacular influences, the example of the Scottish baronial style, and the contemporary fashion for Arts and Crafts. In this event he restored the house with a light touch bringing to the fore its authentic and original style while,

simultaneously, he formalised the gardens and designed furniture to trace the exterior style into the interior design. His design for the restoration is a classic architectural drawing of its type displaying a carefully notated plan and façade elevation with an overview of the house and garden.

Robert Lorimer would go on to have a glittering career culminating in his design for the Scottish National War Memorial that sits, at the highest point, in the grounds of Edinburgh Castle. His elder brother John Henry Lorimer was an academician (RSA 1900) who lived at Kellie Castle and was a renowned painter of domestic scenes and portraits. And Robert's son, Hew Lorimer, would become an eminent sculptor whose best known work is, perhaps, the monumental *Our Lady of the Isles* located on the island of South Uist.

The significance of Robert Lorimer's diploma submission, however, is located in the sense of a melding of traditional themes with an Arts and Crafts sensibility that prioritised notions of simplicity, authenticity and formal consistency. Increasingly these would become key themes of the modern artists working in Scotland.

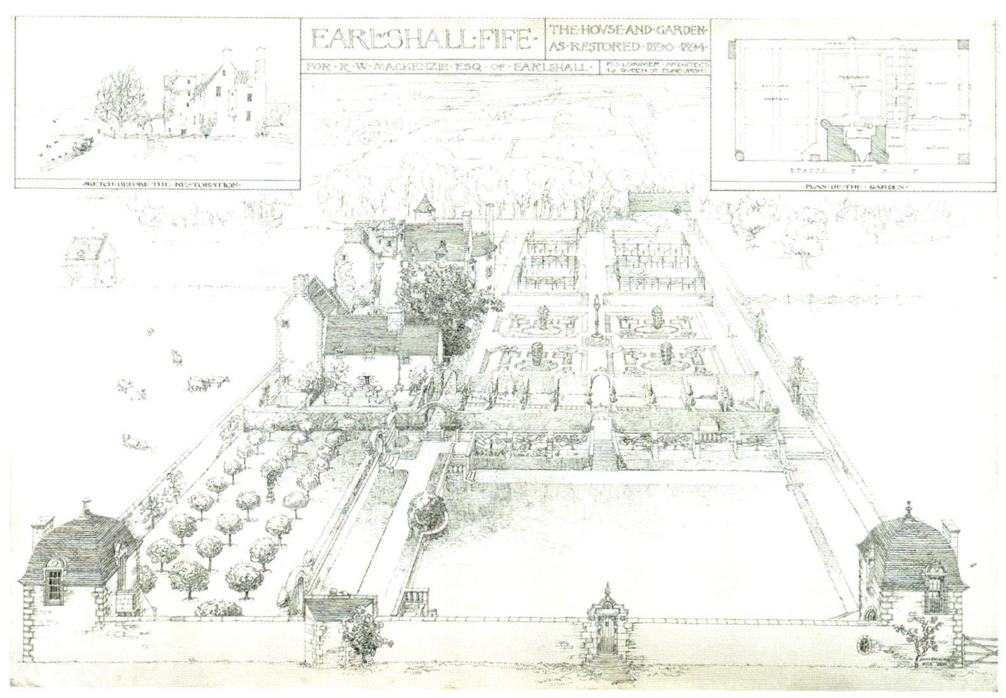

Robert Lorimer, Earlshall, Fife the house and garden as restored 1890–1894 for R W Mackenzie Esq of Earlshall
Drawing by John Begg, 1895

Modernism, in all its multifaceted manners, would appear and develop in the academy during the 1890s. Given the time-frame, and the nature of the institution, this modernism was not an experimental symbolism nor a novel aestheticism but it was a measured innovation. Significantly, this more experimental manner was initiated by artists from Glasgow and the west of Scotland.

James Guthrie (1859–1930) was a prominent member of the 'Glasgow Boys' and so an advocate of naturalism, and even realism, that would eventually be tempered into an uncompromising Impressionism. It was not without controversy when he was elected an associate member of the academy in 1888 and the then President, Sir William Fettes Douglas, was recorded as saying 'these Glasgow fellows are very troublesome. They have their own Institution. What do they want here, at all? If they are hung badly here in Edinburgh, I am sorry for it, but we must look after ourselves' (Gordon 157). Fettes Douglas was renown for his less than diplomatic speech-making, but Guthrie's election as a full academician in 1892 was a signal of the modernisation of the academy. The ultimate irony, of course, was that Guthrie would eventually inherit Fettes Douglas' role as President in 1902 – following the Presidency of George Reid – and would hold that office until 1919.

Guthrie's diploma submission remains one of the most popular works in the collection. At the point when Guthrie was elected a full academician his career as an innovator in painting method was largely behind him. In the early 1880s he had explored the searing realism of *A Funeral Service in the Highlands* and *The Hind's Daughter* as well as the *plein-air* technique of *Hard at it*. From 1890 his reputation rested on his skill as a portrait painter and this was to be his vocation until his death in 1930, but *Midsummer* was a kind of homage to his years of experiment. Impressionist in style and in subject the painting shows a group of three women, evidently bourgeois in dress and demeanour, taking tea in a garden. Under the canopy of a tree the dappled sunlight bounces across their dresses, the foliage, and the garden lawn. In high-keyed colour the artist's touch creates patterns that echo the sense of shifting light on surface that was the epitome of an impressionist style. The purple shadow and stippled highlights perfectly recall the sense of a summer's day.

Midsummer is a scene of leisure and modern manners that reflects upon the nature of a changing social landscape: one in which a contemporary middle-class, socially progressive and economically dominant, begins to visualise its position in the modern world. In this sense it is a more 'radical' painting than its comfortable and charming demeanour might presume.

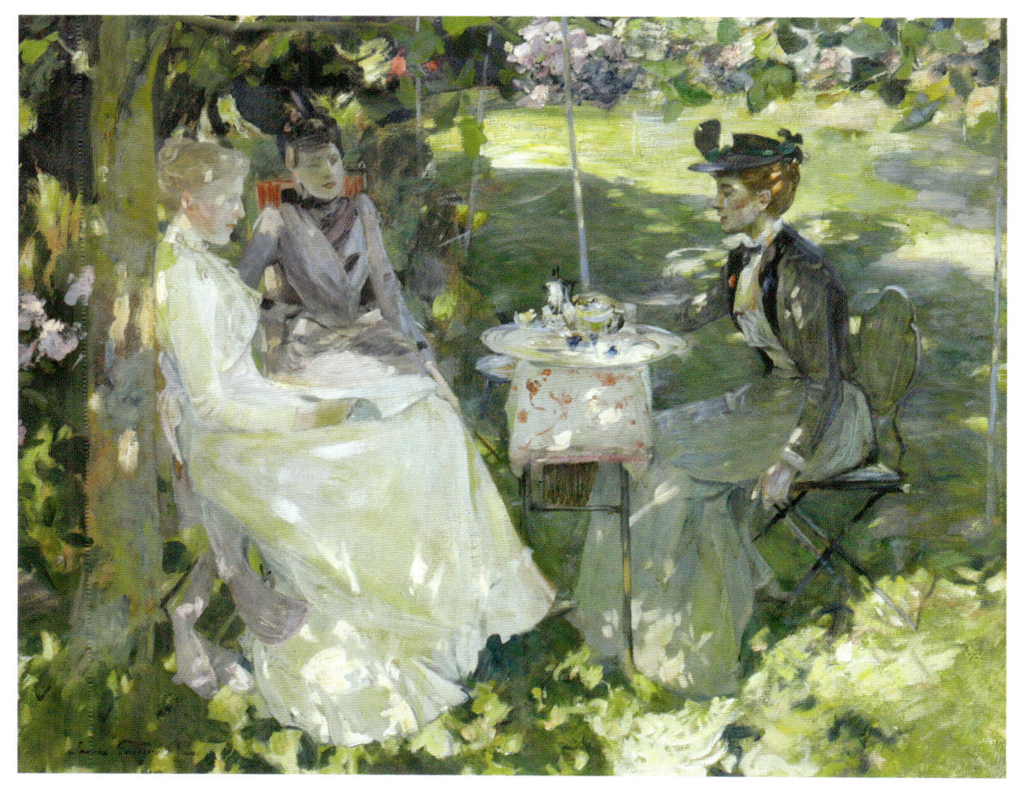

James Guthrie, *Midsummer*

EDWARD ARTHUR WALTON, *The Portfolio*

The sense of a changing social landscape at the end of the 19th century was evidenced in a host of innovations and contemporary themes that began to percolate through the academy. In fact the mood of 'modernity' slowly filled the halls of the institution.

Edward Arthur Walton (1860–1922) was a close friend and associate of James Guthrie and, like him, a significant figure in the Glasgow School. Like Guthrie, also, he had little formal training, though he had spent some time in the mid and late 1870s studying in Dusseldorf and at Glasgow School of Art. His most innovative work helped define the character of Scottish impressionism and was undertaken alongside Guthrie in Glasgow and at Cockburnspath in East Lothian. Here they, jointly, melded the naturalism of the genre tradition with the subdued impressionism of Jules Bastein-Lepage and would eventually create a modern impressionism that was fully realised in works like Walton's *En Plein Air*, completed in Helensburgh during 1885.

Walton was also a champion of James Abbot MacNeill Whistler and the accent of Whistler's aestheticism and technique is marked in his diploma submission *The Portfolio*. Walton was elected a full academician in 1905 by which point he had settled to a professional career as a portrait painter in Edinburgh. But he had, during the 1890s, been a member of the artistic set that inhabited Cheyne Walk in Chelsea and so the bravado impressionism of that group – Whistler, Philip Wilson Steer,

et.al. – determined the 'look' of his diploma work. It was also, evidently, shaped by the fashion for Velasquez's painting that was being cultivated by R.A.M. Stevenson, the cousin of the great poet, who published his homily to the Spanish master in 1895.

The Portfolio, however, is interesting for other reasons. It depicts a female artist, pen in hand, reflecting upon a portfolio of prints and drawings. Walton's sister, Constance, was an artist, as was his wife Helen Law. His daughter, Cecile Walton, would become a key figure in the development of Scottish Symbolism during the early years of the 20th century and the representation of a woman artist in *The Portfolio* projects the emerging importance of women artists in the contemporary scene. Indeed Fiona MacSporran in her book 'Edward Arthur Walton' identifies the sitter as the young Cecile, aged 13.

In fact this image might be viewed, in parallel with Guthrie's leisured middle-class women in *Midsummer*, as a recognition of the changing role of women at the turn of the century: a developing era of the 'new freewoman', of the call for suffrage, and of an embryonic liberation. Even within the halls of the academy.

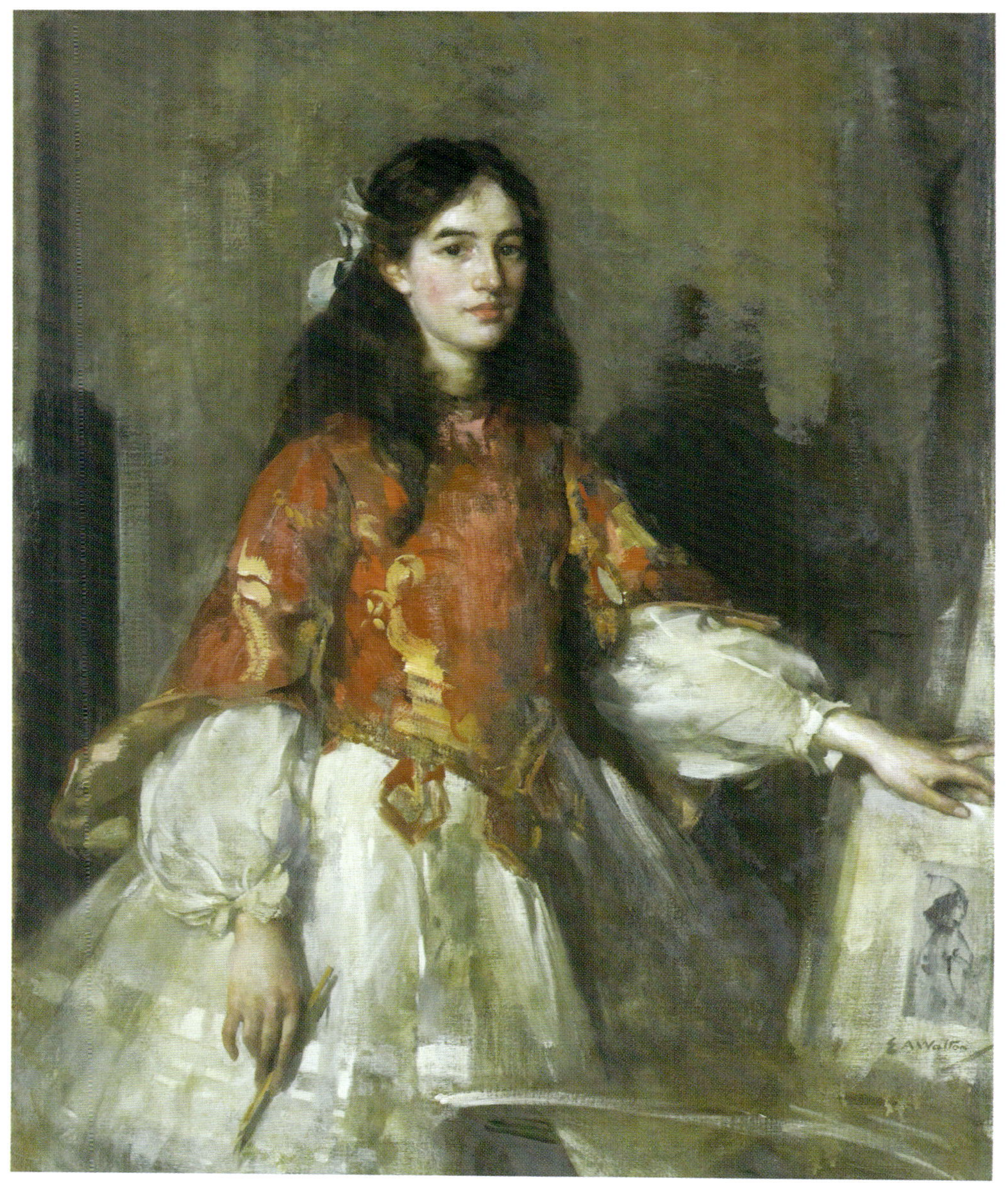

Edward Arthur Walton, *The Portfolio*

JAMES PATERSON, *A Dream of the Nor'
Loch and Edinburgh Castle*

Writing in 1825, at the point when the
academy was coming into being, the
esteemed author and publisher Robert
Chambers remarked in his 'Traditions of
Edinburgh' that 'he who now sees the wide
hollow space between the Old and New
Towns, occupied by beautiful gardens,
having their continuity only somewhat
curiously broken up by a transverse
earthen mound and a line of railway, must
be at a loss to realise the idea of the same
space presenting in former times a lake'.
Chamber's was referring to the Nor' Loch,
or North Loch, that lay at the foot of Castle
Rock and 'was regarded as a portion of the
physical defences of the city'.

The Nor' Loch was drained in 1759 in
order to afford the development of the
New Town, to the north of the castle,
and its environs became the world renown
Princes Street Gardens: adjacent to the
Royal Scottish Academy and the site of
John Steell's statue of Walter Scott,
housed in its Gothic monument.

James Paterson's (1854–1932) remarkable
painting *A Dream of the Nor' Loch and
Edinburgh Castle* was submitted as his
diploma work upon his election to the
academy in 1910, but was painted in 1904.
Paterson had also been a member of the
Glasgow School and he was most closely
associated with the coterie around William
Yorke MacGregor. His most characteristic
work was a subtle, subdued and impres-
sionistic landscape *The Last Turning, Winter,
Moniaive*, painted in Galloway during 1885.

From 1905 he was wholly resident in
Edinburgh and painted many views of the
city as well as recording its most eminent
figures in portraits. His *A Dream of the Nor'
Loch and Edinburgh Castle* is, however,
uncharacteristic and exceptional: the castle
in ruins, the loch a still grey-green wash,
the mood both mysterious and desolate.
In period this dreamscape is really quite
unconventional for it seems to offer a
meditation on deep history – the castle
pre-existing the city – but it remains
ambiguous enough to present the
possibility of a vision of a much-changed
future world. It cannot be viewed as a
'modern' work but it does conjure with
ideas of Symbolism and with the psycho-
logical interpretation of reality that
acknowledged the esoteric realm of human
cognisance and explored the realms of
fantastic metaphor. In this sense, at least,
it might be construed as a dimension of
European Symbolism and an ally to the
Aesthetic Movement in London.

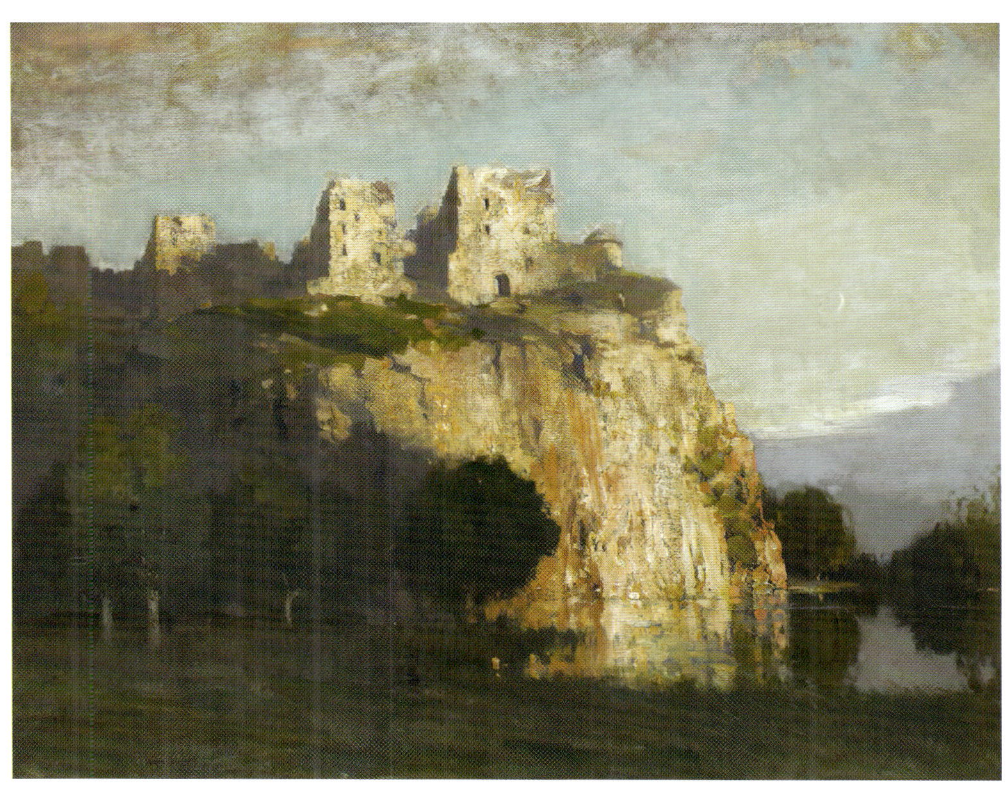

James Paterson, *A Dream of the Nor' Loch and Edinburgh Castle*

HENRY LINTOTT, *Avatar*

Symbolism, of a sort, may also been seen in the work of William Stewart MacGeorge (RSA 1910) who produced a spectral vision of Halloween for his diploma submission, and of Charles Hodge Mackie (RSA 1917) with his *La Danse du Village*. But an extraordinary example of Scottish Symbolism was presented by the otherwise reserved Henry Lintott (1877–1965) upon his election as an academician in 1923.

Lintott's *Avatar* was painted seven years prior to his full election as an academician, in 1916. Evidently, then, it relates to the carnage of the First World War. Lintott was born in England but wholly resident in Edinburgh from the age of 25 and so was eligible for election to the Royal Scottish Academy. His move to Edinburgh was facilitated by an appointment to teach at the newly established Edinburgh College of Art.

The date of this ethereal painting, 1916, signals the mood and intention of what remains an otherworldly image. Esme Gordon records that 'When the 91st Annual Report was submitted by the Council to members, the Great War was over. But, the account was retrospective, the activities noted having occurred during the last year of the holocaust. The gods appear to have smiled on the RSA – although there is no telling how many potential recruits to Associate rank may have forfeited their lives... at least there was in the membership no loss; the Academy is without a War Memorial' (Gordon 184). The fact that no members 'forfeited their lives' may be testament to the senior age of the academicians, but there is a sense in which Lintott provided a memorial for the fallen. *Avatar*, an image of transposition and ascendance, depicts a symbolic warrior, with sword clasped to breast, carried heavenward by four spirit figures. The transient corpse is borne on a travoy, or stretcher. Despite the title this is a patently Christian symbolism with dead figure and sword connoting the image of St Michael and the pallbearers referencing the vision of angels. The painting itself is spiritual and elegiac. A soft, pink and lilac flurry of clouds, the diaphanous robes of the pallbearers, the funeral black fall of the shroud. Lintott, in selecting and presenting his diploma work, was surely recognizing, within the walls of the academy, the unimaginable cost in human life that was the First World War.

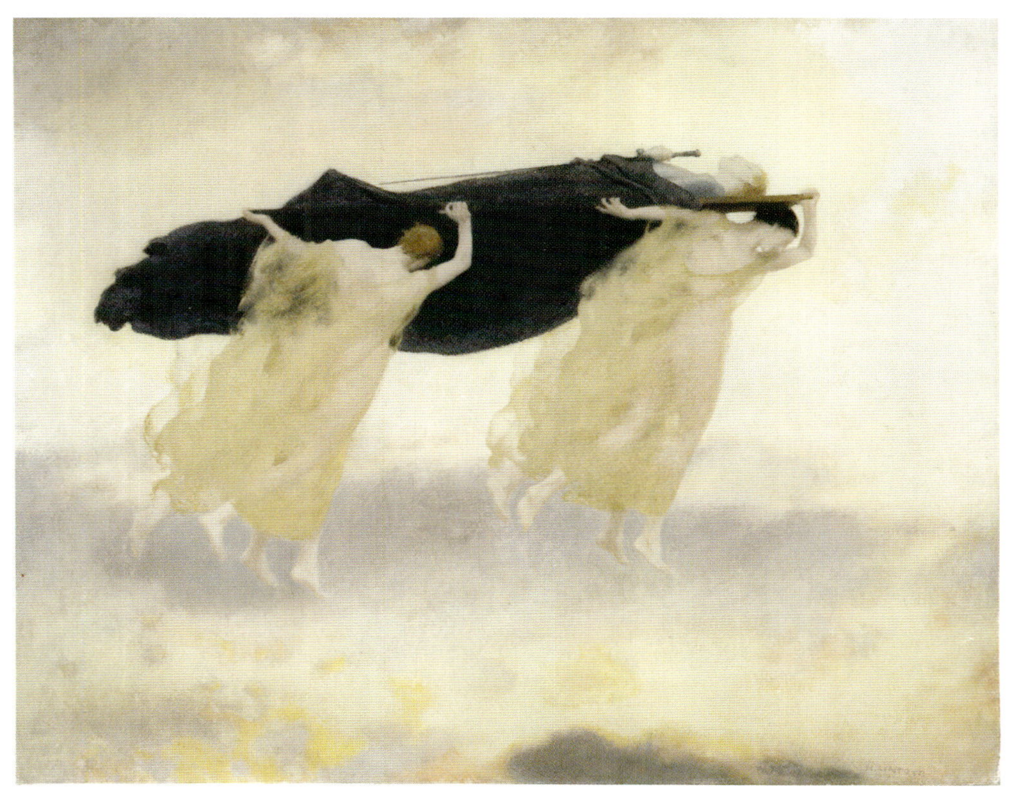

Henry Lintott, *Avatar*

JOHN DUNCAN, *Ivory, Apes and Peacocks*

Henry Lintott's work was certainly symbolic, but the ethos of Scottish Symbolism was surely defined by the aesthetics and career of John Duncan (1866–1945). Elected as an academician in 1923 Duncan provided a signature work *Ivory, Apes and Peacocks* from the same year.

Duncan's diploma work was 'signature' in its technique and its form. He worked largely in tempera and enjoyed the flat, decorative quality of the medium that intensified his fascination with the mural form. The subject of the work, however, was marginal to his more typical imagery for Duncan made his reputation as an advocate for the Celtic Revival. In this pursuit Duncan was a close associate of the botanist and polymath Patrick Geddes; he would help illustrate Geddes' epoch defining journal 'Evergreen' in the mid 1890s, and, in the same decade, he provided murals for Geddes' home in Ramsay Garden and for Ramsay Lodge. In these works he conjured with Celtic themes and symbols and so helped promote a subtle 'nationalist' agenda that reflected upon the deep culture of Scotland. This would extend into typical tempera works like *The Riders of the Sidhe* and *The Children of Lyr* that explored the mythic elements of Celtic lore.

John Tonge has remarked that 'There is, in point of fact, nothing very Celtic about Mr Duncan's paintings, apart from the occasional use of patterns derived from old Celtic ornament and the choice of stories from the classical cycles: Celtic art was abstract, non-humanist and severe; and his, humanist and sentimental. The immediate pictorial influences were Botticelli and Puvis de Chavannes...' (Tonge 93). Certainly the tempera based mural technique was derived from the Italian quattrocento and the symbolist style of Puvis de Chavannes is evident in Duncan's work, but his association with Geddes was part of a genuine search for an 'authentic' national culture that would resonate deep into the 20th century.

Ivory, Apes and Peacocks however, is a decorative scheme from the 1920s that uses the platform of the biblical story – The Queen of Sheba arrives in Israel with precious gifts for Solomon – to present a pot-pourri of naked figures, exotic animals, jewels and decorations that perform a processional dance of sensual and erotic delights. A counterpoint, perhaps, to the presbyterian consciousness and a provocative stimulus in the collection of the academy.

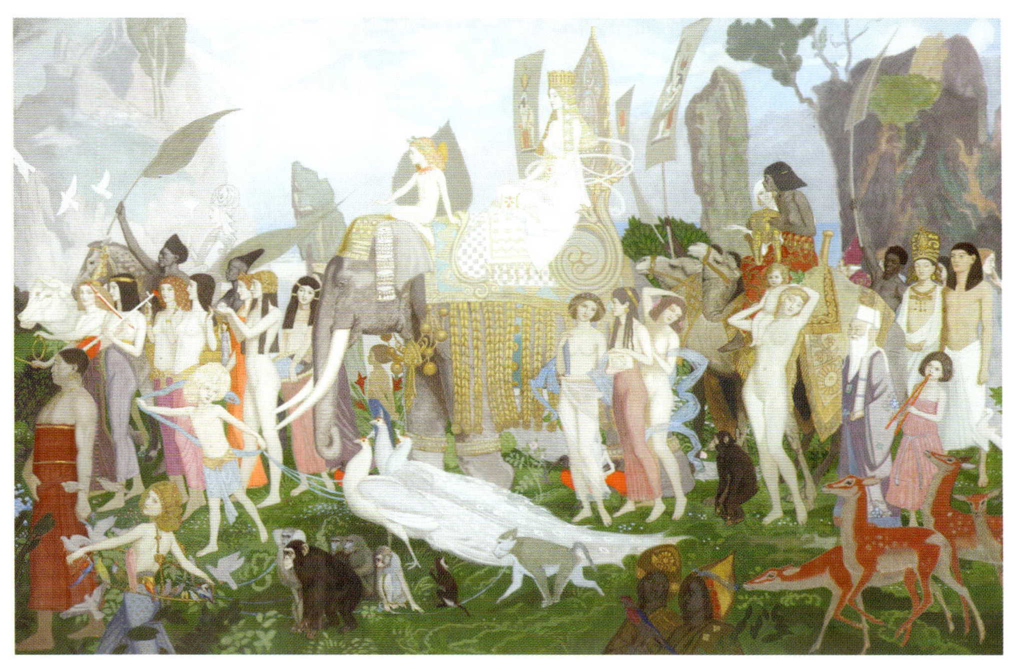

John Duncan, *Ivory, Apes and Peacocks*

SAMUEL JOHN PEPLOE, *Boy Reading*

FRANCIS CAMPBELL BOILEAU CADELL,
The Poet

John Duncan would be considered something of a 'Modern' in Scotland but when elected an academician, in 1923, his most productive and interesting years were behind him – in fact they belonged to the previous century. Modernism itself was, perhaps unsurprisingly, not realised on the academy's walls in this period. For, though the continental avant-gardes were experimenting with Cubist and neo-Cubist form and with every variety of expressionism, they did so in defiance of academic technique. In fact the lag between aesthetic experiment and academic recognition was, where it was sometimes overcome, somewhere between 20 and 30 years.

Most Scottish 'Modernists' had eschewed the academy and even the country. William McCance and William Johnstone working in London, and John Duncan Fergusson living and working in France. Scottish modernism had, of course, taken the particular form of a Fauve inspired 'colourism', and whereas Fergusson would remain, until 1939, a continental artist, his collaborators as 'Scottish Colourists' Samuel Peploe (1871–1935) and Francis Caddell (1883–1937) were both resident Scots and would become academicians.

Given Samuel Peploe's reputation as an adventurous 'modern' and an extravagant colourist it is surprising that his diploma work should be a muted portrait study in tones of grey. Elected an academician in 1927 it is the case that his signature still-lifes and landscapes – much influenced by expressionist colour and Japonisme, and even with some decorative Cubist modulation – had been created in previous decades, but he remained an audacious painter. His *Boy Reading*, in fact his son – William Peploe, in the distinctive school uniform of the Edinburgh Academy – is a subtle and meditative study, the brushwork bold and even daring, but the subject cool and detached.

Francis Cadell's diploma work was, likewise, a portrait study and so equally far removed from his intensely coloured and highly decorative Edinburgh interiors and certainly detached from his joyous landscapes of Iona. Cadell, like Peploe, was late in being admitted to the academy – in 1935 and only two years before his death – but his diploma work, *The Poet*, was a piece of bravura painting from the pre-war period. The sitter is Norman MacDonald, sometimes known as Herman MacDonald, and he is draped across a sofa in a shambolic studio – it is a both a study of Edinburgh bohemia and a celebration of the freely-painted open brushwork that was the best of Cadell's early years.

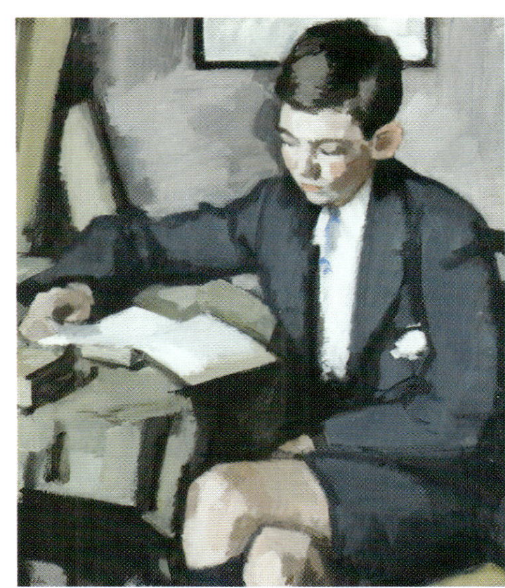

Samuel John Peploe, *Boy Reading*

Francis Campbell Boileau Cadell, *The Poet*

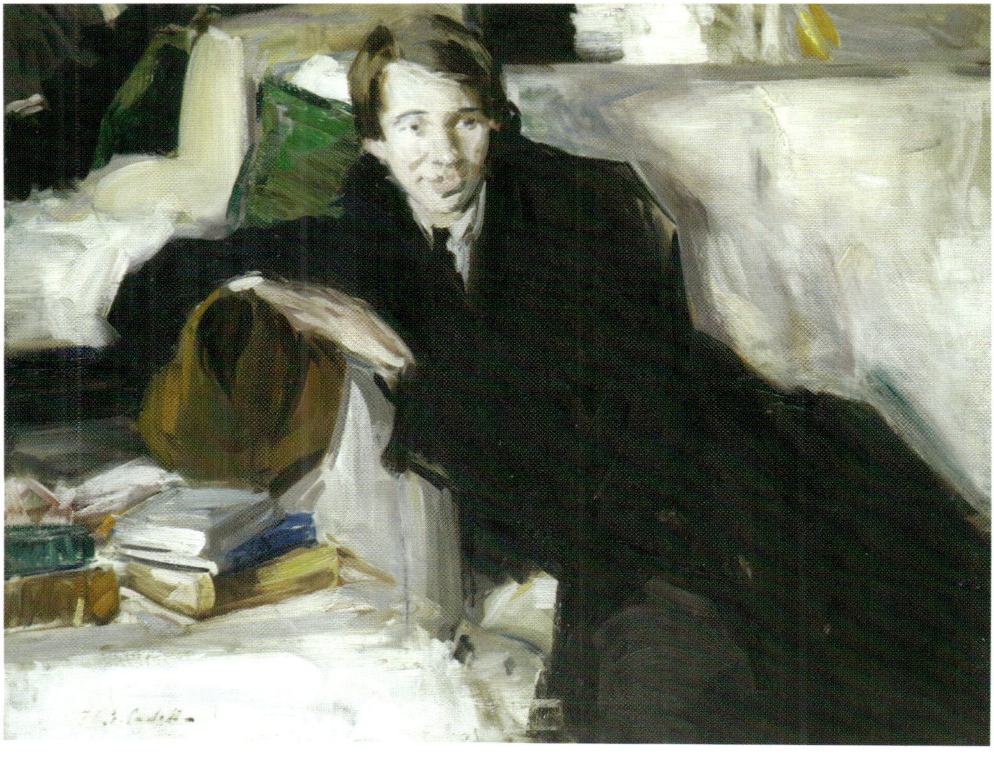

WILLIAM OLIPHANT HUTCHISON,
Portrait of James Gunn

Portraiture was an important outlet for painters during the economically turbulent inter-war years, and Scottish academicians developed a particular skill for this genre. None more so than William Oliphant Hutchison (1889–1970) who was first elected to the academy in 1943 and would become its President from 1950 until 1959.

Hutchison's diploma submission, the *Portrait of James Gunn*, is typical in its academic manner and dark tonality. But, the austerity, the rigour, the sombre and understated demeanour give a substance and a presence to the sitter that is remarkable. The sitter, James Gunn, was himself a noted portrait painter and both men were decidedly 'establishment': their sitters included royalty, aristocrats and the most powerful individuals of their age. But their background and history is interesting. Hutchison had been a founder member of The Edinburgh Group, established in 1912 and representing a bohemian wellspring in the capital city. In his catalogue for a retrospective on the group Jake Kemplay quotes a reviewer of the period, Fredric Quinton, 'In the New Gallery, at Shandwick Place... we have found something... of pagan brazenness rather than parlour propriety. Half Edinburgh goes to Shandwick Place secretly desiring to be righteously shocked' (Kemplay 7). Alongside Hutchison in The Edinburgh Group there was Eric Robertson, an extraordinary modern painter, and also Robertson's esteemed partner Cecile Walton (Hutchison would marry Cecile Walton's sister, Margery, and so become E.A. Walton's son-in-law). Hutchison would, in this period, travel to Paris where he met with James Gunn and they were friends thereafter. Both men had difficulties while serving during the First World War, and both would have significant careers in London as portrait painters – indeed both were knighted.

Hutchison moved to Glasgow to become Director of Glasgow School of Art in 1932 and retired to Edinburgh in 1943. But the portraiture of Hutchison and Gunn, particularly in their private works, often painting one another or in self-portraits, is unnerving and mysterious. They both have a facility to execute dark and brooding portraits; presences that substantiate the nature of the sitter in paint yet explore the existential conditions of being in a manner that borders upon the uncanny. The *Portrait of James Gunn* is exemplary in this respect for Hutchison has balanced the sullen and downcast face of the sitter against the gloved hat and cane, and the polished top hat, in a dramatic formal arrangement that accents the characteristics of a saturnine and tragic melancholy.

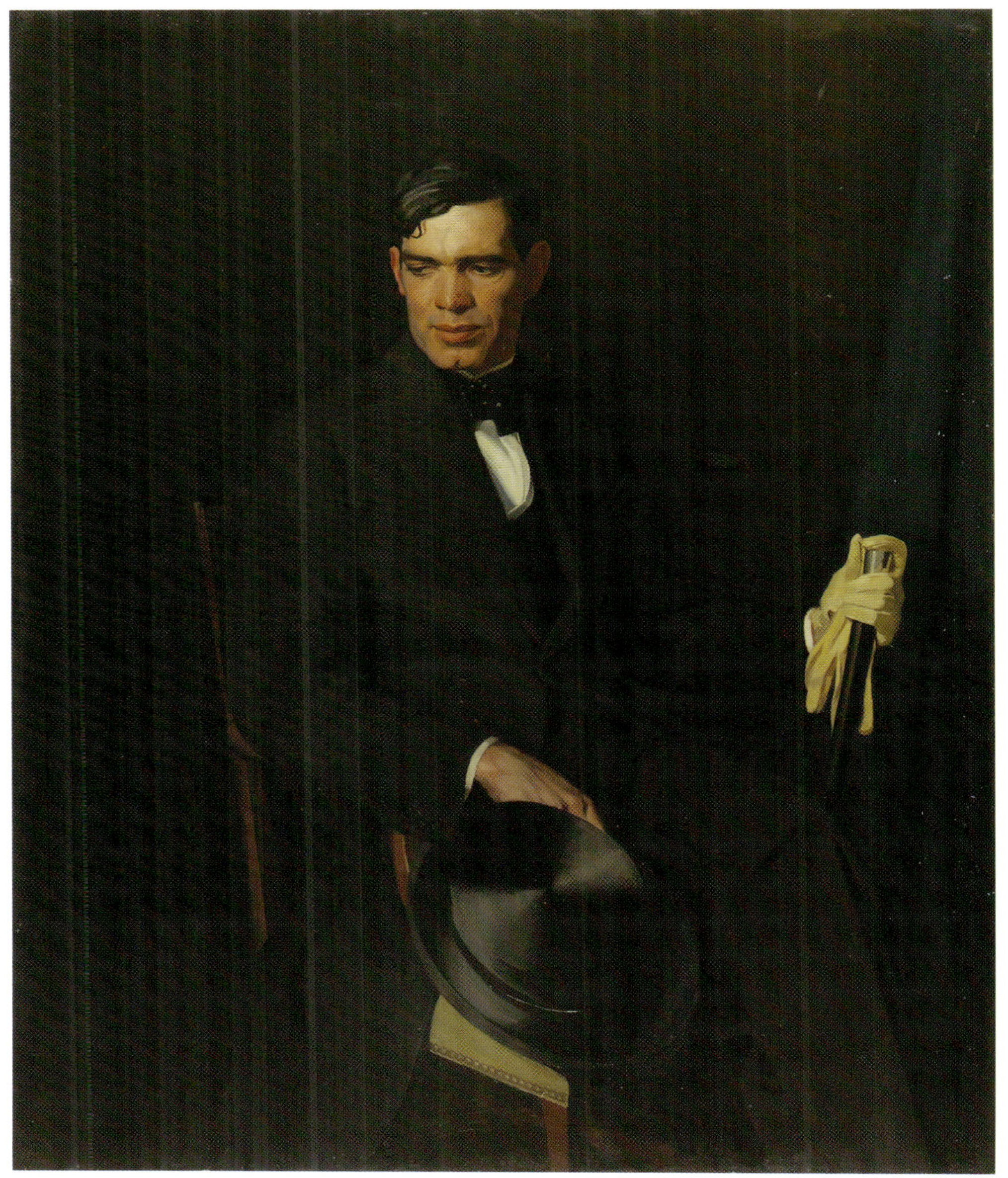

William Oliphant Hutchison, *Portrait of James Gunn*

JAMES COWIE, *Miss Barbara Graham Cowie*

ROBERT SIVELL, *Portrait of Hamish Paterson*

Portraits, in all their many guises, were and are a feature of the diploma collection. James Cowie (1886–1956) was elected an academician in 1943, but his careful technique was based on a dedicated study of the Italian *quattrocento* manner, and was an established academic approach. A meticulous and painstaking craftsman he completed many detailed drawings of his subjects prior to working on the final image. Committed to work in teaching – first at Bellshill Academy and subsequently at Gray's School of Art in Aberdeen – his subjects were principally his students, in groups and singly. But his diploma work was a finely worked and sensitive portrait of his youngest daughter, Barbara. A full figure study, with the young girl looking directly at the viewer, and surrounded by household paraphernalia of chair and curtains and book and painting, this is an archetypal example of Cowie's unique style; familiar in its subject but strangely detached in its atmosphere.

Cowie's contemporary Robert Sivell (1888–1958) had, likewise, journeyed from Glasgow to teach in Aberdeen and would be elected an academician in the same year as Cowie. Both men presented a certain formality in their work though Sivell's diploma submission, a *Portrait of Hamish Paterson*, has a looser and more expressive quality more in keeping with the *belle painter* tradition. Hamish Paterson was in fact Sivell's contemporary, the landscape and portrait painter James Constable Paterson, who was a son of James Paterson RSA. Universally known as Hamish, he is shown bowing a single string fiddle held between his knees. A vernacular and even a folksy portrait it has a colloquial quality that counters the official world of the academy.

Interestingly these portraits, submitted as diploma works, were of family and friends. This was, and became, something of a trope. Evidently E.A. Walton, Samuel Peploe and W.O. Hutchison all presented images of family and friends. Later, Donald Moodie, elected an academician 1952, presented a brightly coloured portrait of his daughter, reading on a sun-speckled beach in Iona, titled *Summer*. And a stream of portrait studies, often informal or decorative or 'modern', would become familiar in the diploma collection. These were substantial works, and presented not simply to 'find a home' for non-commercial paintings, but as personal tributes, fond recollections and memorials that might be given an official and permanent status.

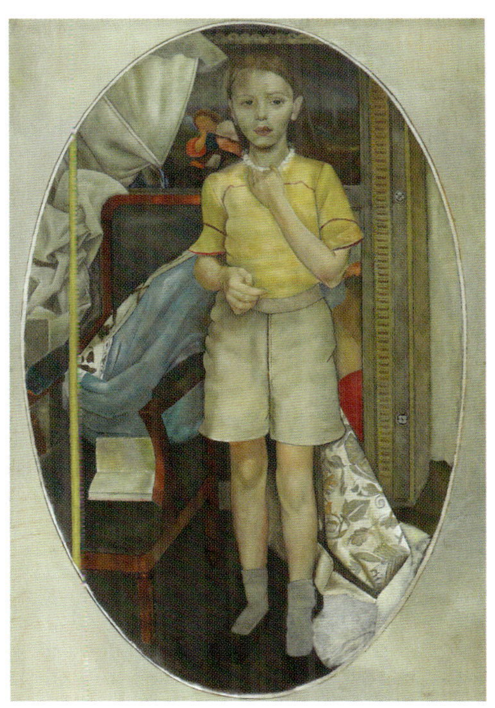

James Cowie, *Miss Barbara Graham Cowie*

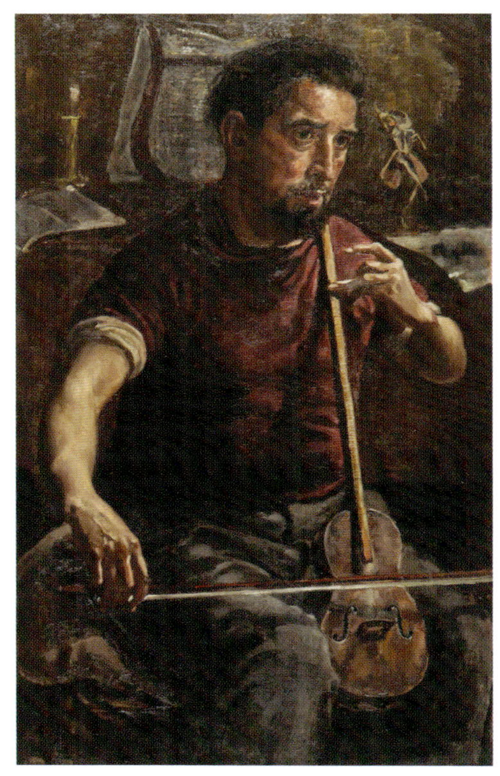

Robert Sivell, *Hamish Paterson*

PHYLLIS MARY BONE, *Shere Khan the Tiger*

Many of these portraits were of women and it might be suggested that this was the only means through which women could have an official status within the academy. Janice Helland, in her study of 'Professional Women Painters in 19th-Century Scotland' has remarked that '… it is significant that women were kept out of the inner circle of the most prestigious of the artists' groups (the Royal Scottish Academy)…' (Helland 7) and it is the case that women were excluded from full academician status throughout the 19th and much of the 20th century. As Helland amply testifies women artists were represented in academy exhibitions, and the history of art by women is a vital and vibrant element in the story of Scotland's art. The academy, however, marginalised women on what were taken to be 'professional' grounds; their marital and domestic roles rendering them unsuitable for the full-time professional activity of artist. This conservatism and sexism, so typical of the political and cultural context of the period, would stain the academy until the period of the Second World War. While some women had previously been accorded associate status (ARSA) it was not until 1944 that a woman would be elected as an academician.

Phyllis Bone (1894–1972) was an established sculptor known for her animal studies. Her most familiar work is presented within the halls of the Scottish National War Memorial, situated in Edinburgh Castle. The Memorial was designed by Robert Lorimer, and under his guidance a number of sculptors and crafts-people produced decorations and ornaments that memorialised all aspects of war service, and the dead of the First World War. Opened in 1927, Bone had provided a lion and unicorn statue for the entrance, but it was her carved stone panel *The Tunnellers' Friends* that was, and is, one of the most popular works in the monument. This low-relief carving depicts a group of caged canaries and three mice within a laurel wreath. Bone was, of course, memorialising the animals that had died while acting as agents for the tunnelling corps; the primary sensors of gas in the underground channels.

When elected a full academician in 1944 Bone donated a typical animal sculpture, this time based upon a figure from Rudyard Kipling's 'Jungle Book'. Shere Khan, the lame tiger, prowls the jungle floor in an extraordinarily animate manner, all determination and anger. The work is characteristic of the facility Bone had for instilling, in her bronze and stone statuary, an extraordinary sentient and living movement.

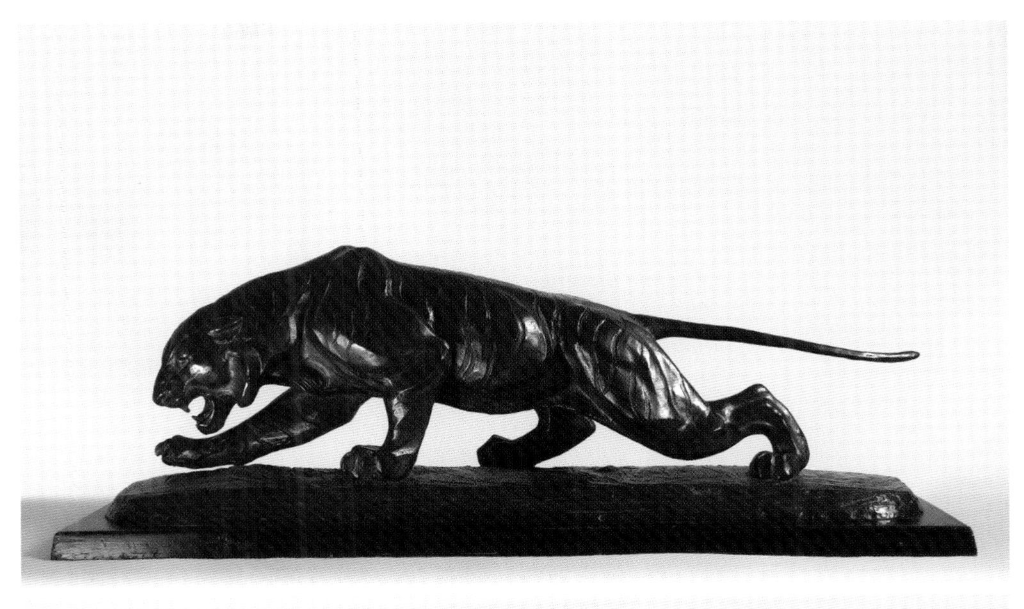

Phyllis Mary Bone, *Shere Khan the Tiger*

ANNE REDPATH, *In the Chapel of St Jean, Tréboul*

Phyllis Bone was the first woman to be given full recognition within the academy and was, strangely, a sculptor. Strangely, for women painters were, by far, the more representative figures in the Scottish art world. It was in 1952, however, that Anne Redpath (1895–1965) became the first woman painter to be given full membership of the academy and so could place the letters RSA after her name.

Redpath was, by the 1950s, one of the key figures within the Edinburgh cultural establishment and a confidant of the elite within the academy. But it was also in the decade of the 1950s that she began to produce some of her most adventurous painting. From a background in the Scottish borders she attended Edinburgh School of Art from 1913 where her tutor would be Henry Lintott, amongst others. Married to the architect James Michie, from 1920, she became a wife and mother and her output as an artist suffered. The family having lived in France, and elsewhere, returned to the border country in 1934 and Redpath was resident in Edinburgh from 1949. This period saw some of her most interesting painting; magnificently textured, often brightly coloured and decorous, Redpath focused on sublime domestic still-lifes and landscape. Following her election to the academy she moved to London Street, in Edinburgh, and this flat would become a favourite Salon for Edinburgh artists and academicians: a phenomenon amply celebrated in Robin Philipson's expressionist memorial painting of

Anne Redpath's House: London Street, which recorded the cream of Edinburgh's artists in conclave and under the guidance of Redpath.

The submission of Redpath's diploma work followed a number of journeys in Spain, France and the Canaries, and is evidence of the experiment and adventure of her later years. *In the Chapel of St Jean, Tréboul* is, evidently, a memory of a journey in Brittany and demonstrates a loosening of technique, a symbolic naivety of style, and an intuitive decorative sensibility that speaks to a studied spontaneity and thoughtful primitivism. That is, she was exploring those avenues of naïve art that looked to replicate the sense of a creative authenticity embedded in instinctive experience. In truth, this manner would become something of a trope within the Edinburgh artists and the academicians of Redpath's circle.

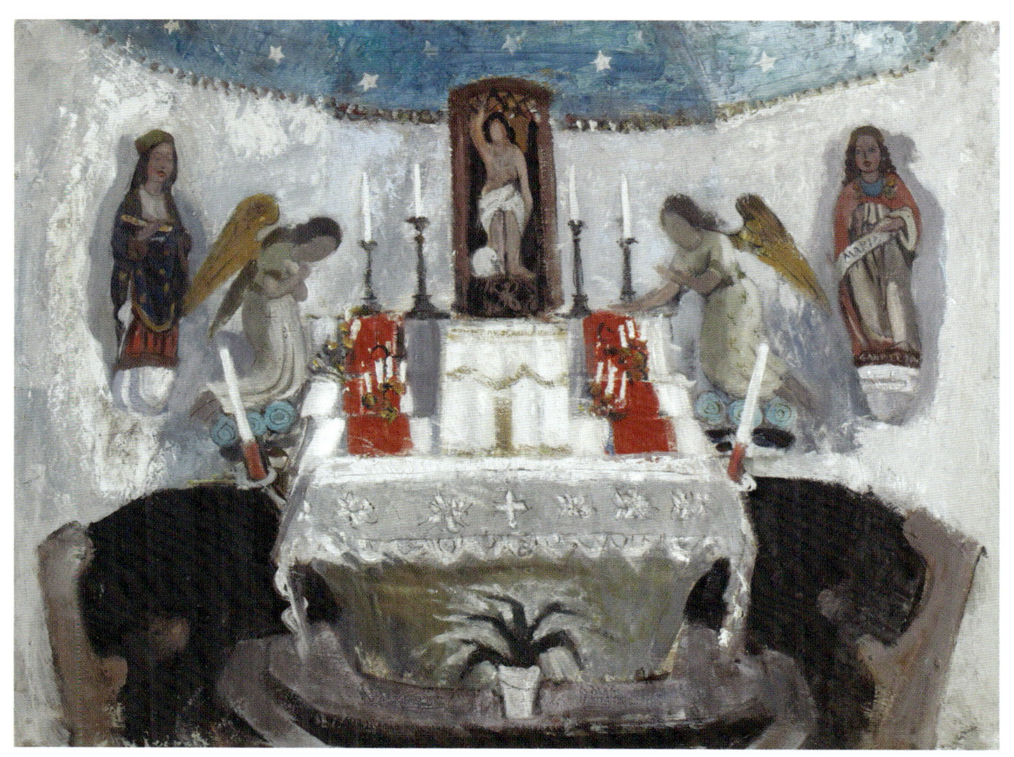

Anne Redpath, *In the Chapel of St Jean, Tréboul*

WILLIAM GILLIES, *Still-life; Yellow Jug and Striped Cloth*

Among Anne Redpath's near contemporaries at Edinburgh College of Art was an individual who would become one of the most influential figures in Scottish art during the 20th century. This is perhaps surprising for William Gillies (1898–1973) was not the most extrovert of men. His studies at the art school had been interrupted by the First World War, and it was 1923 before he travelled to Paris to study with Andre L'hote. Here he absorbed many of the lessons of L'hote's 'Salon Cubism'. He would, in the pattern of so many Scottish artists, return to Edinburgh School of Art to teach and became both Head of Painting, in 1946, and Principal of the college, in 1959. It was in these roles that he would influence generations of Scottish artists and shape the 'manner' of Edinburgh painting.

His work, mainly landscape and still-life painting, would develop in a loose and expressive manner and could shift from the near abstract to the profoundly linear and representative. Keith Hartley in 'Scottish Art since 1900' has remarked that 'In his best work he simplified and omitted detail, concentrating on shapes as they appeared flat of the canvas' (Hartley 33), and this is certainly the case in his magnificent watercolour *Skye Hills near Morar* and indeed in the many landscapes he painted following his retreat to the Midlothian countryside in 1939.

Gillies was made a member of the academy in 1947, the first of many honours that would culminate in his knighthood.

Duncan Macmillan in 'Scottish Art in the 20th Century' comments that 'In still-life especially, he was sometimes a little fantastic and occasionally too obviously beholden to French models at the expense of his own individuality' (Macmillan, SATC, 68), and so it may be considered odd that he chose to present *Still-life; Yellow Jug and Striped Cloth* as his diploma piece. Certainly the 'French model' is manifest in this painting. There is a decorative component to the composition, the table-top is tipped towards the picture plain, blocks of vibrant colour accentuate a shallow picture space. In fact it carries much of the import of a 'Salon Cubism' filtered through the technical innovation of late Cezanne. But it might also be viewed as a kind of manifesto piece. Pictures within the picture reference the fascinating harbour scenes he painted from the 1930s, flat blocks of colour allude to the abstract quality of his 'simplified' landscape views, the passages of scrubbed brushwork indicate his fascination with a restrained expressionist technique, and, the shadow still-life – on the right of the painting – positions his art within the context of European modernism. It was, to a large extent, these qualities that made him such an influential figure, within Edinburgh, within the academy, and within British art more generally.

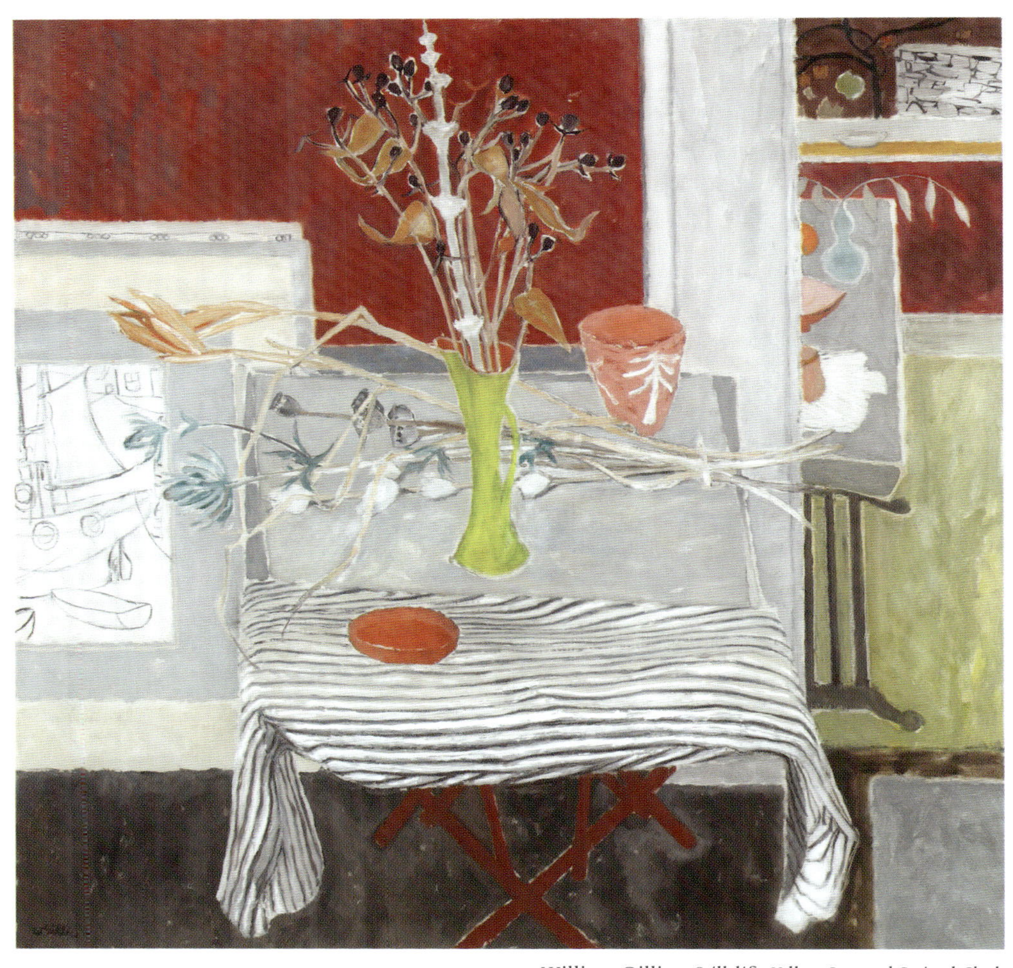

William Gillies, *Still-life; Yellow Jug and Striped Cloth*

JOHN MAXWELL, *The Bull*

William Gillies' fellow traveller, on his painting trips to the Highlands of Scotland and to the East Neuk of Fife, was the eminent, in fact fascinating, symbolist John Maxwell (1905–1962). Maxwell's diploma work, following his admission to the academy in 1949, was the oil painting *The Bull*, a raw and extraordinarily hostile image. Extraordinary, for Maxwell was a reserved and gentle man whose work had an ethereal quality and was often completed in watercolour, or as meticulous and sometimes whimsical ink drawings, or in gouache. In fact his training at Edinburgh College of Art overlapped with Gillies, and like Gillies and Redpath he would travel on the continent to absorb the lessons of modernism. His greatest debt was to the French symbolists and it is generally acknowledged that he moved between the influences of Odilon Redon and the Russian émigré Marc Chagall.

The Bull is a symbolist work but not in the manner of Maxwell's signature paintings, nor his fairytale drawings. Mostly, Maxwell would conjure a kind of dreamscape populated by young women in diaphanous gowns, clouds of fragile flowers, nightbirds and moonlit scenes; his work had a fantasy element, and a pensive quality. *The Bull* is visceral and primeval and an instinctual piece of painting. There is a fascinating reel of film held in the Scottish Screen Archive. It is titled 'Three Scottish Painters' and was directed by Laurence Henson for the Scottish Arts Council. Released in the year after Maxwell's death it, nevertheless, shows the artist at work in his home studio. Maxwell is using a palette-knife, he lifts paint from a thickly layered palette and applies it to a canvas depicting fish. The image is a kind of primordial world, a sub-aqueous species memory. But Maxwell is careful to create texture and facture on the canvas. There is pattern, certainly, but the image is created through the impasto nature of the surface. This, too, is the manner of his diploma work. *The Bull* emerges from a scrubbed and course background, patches of red and lilac rub up against greys and black, the work is all gesture and intensity. Of course the symbol of the bull is masculine and sexual, and something of this is reflected in the raw green and red eyes of the animal, but throughout there exists a kind of repressed anger in the painting.

In all these respects Maxwell's diploma submission was slightly askew from the general tenor of his painting. However, the expressionism of the painting, the scoured and textured surface of the work, would become a feature of Edinburgh painting, and so of academic art, in the period after the Second World War.

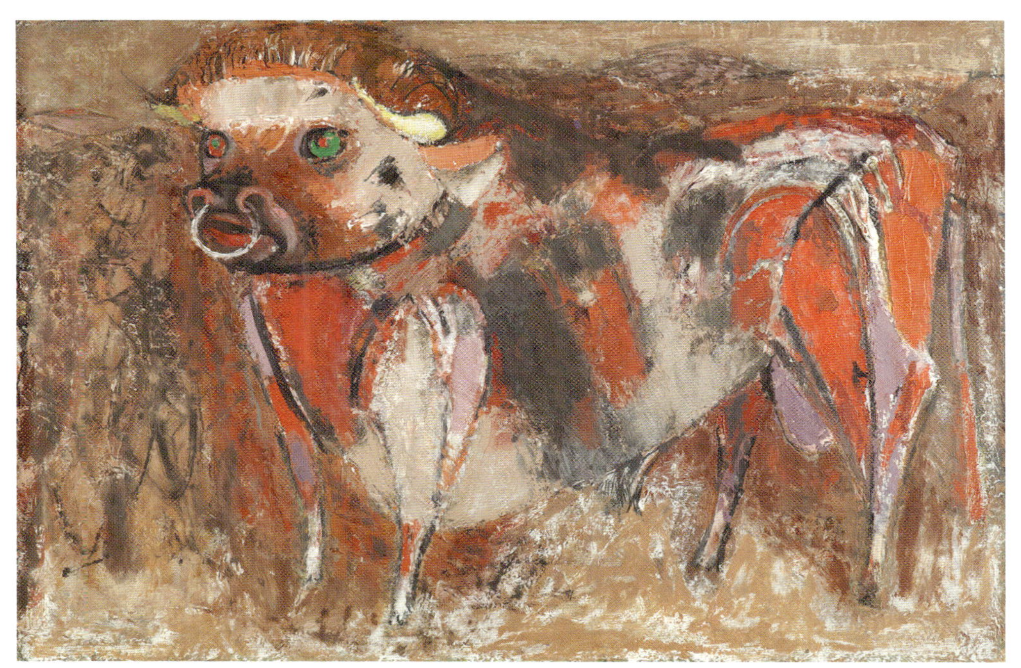

John Maxwell, *The Bull*

The trinity of the Edinburgh Salons, Edinburgh College of Art, and the Royal Scottish Academy became fully established in the post-war period, and was a kind of hegemony. Certainly the two most influential Presidents of the academy at this time were both denizens of that privileged network.

William MacTaggart (1903–1981) was the grandson of Scotland's greatest landscape painter William McTaggart (RSA 1870) and had lifelong friendships with Redpath, Gillies and Maxwell. He both attended and taught at Edinburgh College of Art and was elected to the academy in 1948. Like Redpath his home, in Drummond Place in Edinburgh, would become a Salon for local artists though he had strong connections with Scandinavia and the South of France. Elected President of the academy in 1959 he would hold this position throughout the turbulent decade of the 1960s and so would be at the centre of the many upheavals that raced through the cultural life of the capital in this time of change and 'counter-culture'. His diploma work *At Longniddry* is typical of his loosely expressionist style. A landscape depicting some cottages in the East Lothian town it echoes some of the concerns of the Scottish Colourists deflected through his abiding interest in the late work of Edvard Munch.

The profile of Robin Philipson (1916–1992) was similar in form and content, though he was effectively a generation after MacTaggart. He completed his training at Edinburgh College of Art in 1940, and naturally became engaged in the war. Subsequently he was a respected tutor at the college and would become Head of Drawing and Painting. Elected to the academy in 1962 he would be President from 1973–1983 and so something of an archetype of the Edinburgh establishment. For all this Philipson's work could contain elements of radicalism and even a quasi-political intent. Certainly he was prone to the decorative, and to the iteration of nude and Odalisque type subjects, but works like *Stone the Crows* could project subtle anti-war themes and his magnificent series of 'Cock Fights' is an object lesson in gestural expressionism. Philipson's diploma piece, *Lament*, contains all of these positive qualities. An abstract style worked through a geometric grid, it hints at narrative scenes that invoke associations with rebellion, containment and mourning. The ambiguity of the work is its great strength, but so is the virtuoso handling of paint and surface, and the subtle sense of colour contrast.

It would be true to say that much of the reputation of the academy has been focussed through the social network the MacTaggart and Philipson came to represent, but the dominance of this group was ready to be challenged.

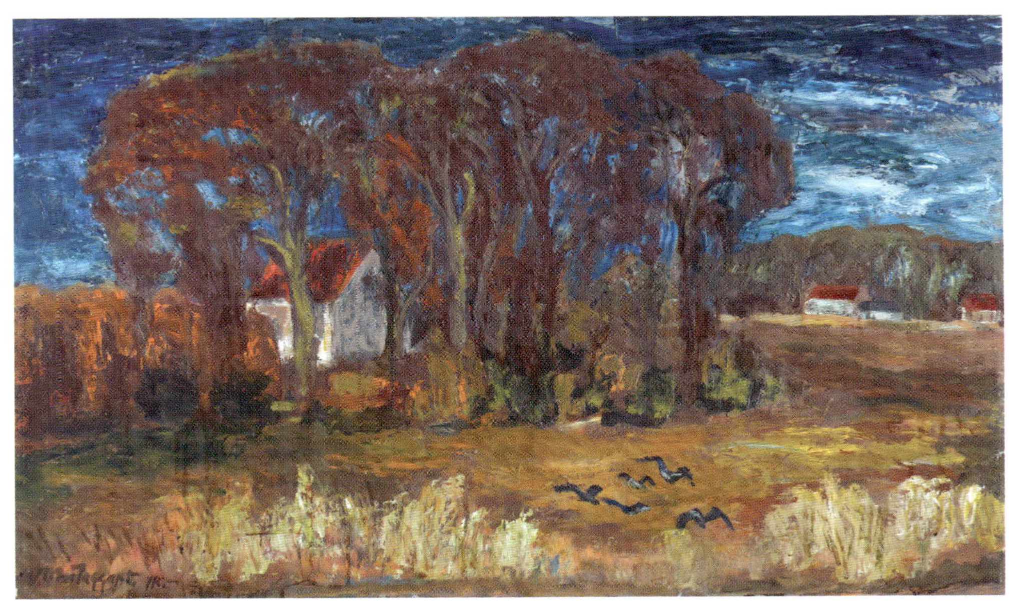

William MacTaggart, *At Longniddry*
(or *After Rain, Longniddry*)

Robin Philipson, *Lament*

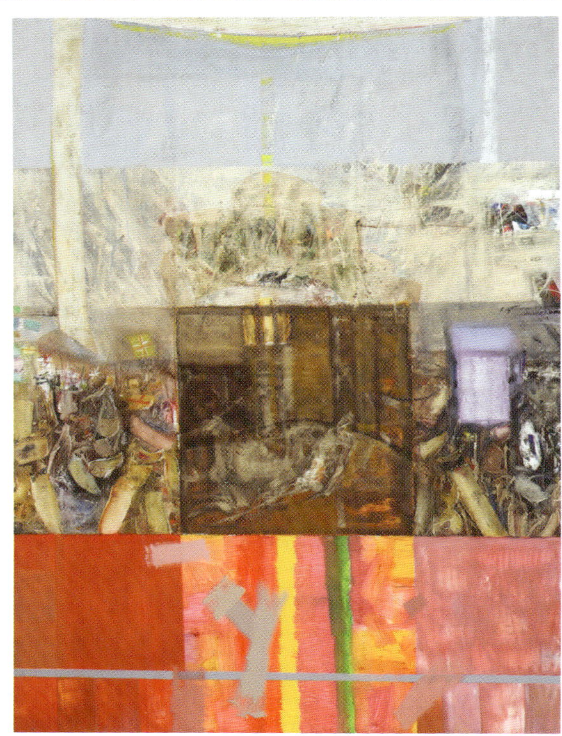

JOAN EARDLEY, *Summer Sea*

Whereas Anne Redpath was the first woman painter to be elected an academician, and was an Edinburgh artist to her core, Joan Eardley (1921–1963) was recognized as a west-coast painter of social subjects and working-class life. Trained at Glasgow School of Art during the war years she would benefit from travel in France and in Italy, following her post-diploma studies, on a scholarship partly funded by the academy.

Eardley's work traversed an arc from Van Gogh to Willem de Kooning, but her vision was a challenge to the salon paintings of the Edinburgh School and the decorative nature of Scottish painting more generally. Having established a studio in the Townhead area of Glasgow she painted, principally, the lives of street-children. Her insistence on the vigour and vitality of working class life extended to a fascination with graffiti and so her images of tenement children were often set against a background of scrawls and writings on the walls of buildings. While her approach to painting often echoed the gestural sweep and rubbed surface of the graffiti style she worked with collaged elements pressed into the painted surface and displayed an expressive manner that responded to the forms of European and American abstraction.

Though Eardley was admired for her daring images of working-class life in the 1950s she also explored the world of landscape painting. This was encouraged by her discovery of Catterline, a small fishing village on the north-east coast of Scotland. From 1952 she would spend the larger part of each year in the village and would paint the seascapes and fields in the immediate environs. These were dynamic and vibrant works, painted directly from nature and incorporating all the elemental force of the world she observed. Often the canvases would evidence the wind-blown sand and sea-spray of the wild shoreline, or she might press into the wet paint the seeds and flowers of the fields.

Although elected an associate of the academy in 1955 she was not elected to full membership until 1963, and this was the year of her death. Her diploma work is one of her finest Catterline seascapes – selected by the RSA from the Joan Eardley Memorial Exhibition held at the Scottish Gallery in 1964, and gifted as her diploma work by the artist's sister, Irene Eardley, on behalf of the family. *Summer Sea* is a painting charged with the physical immediacy of having been painted directly from nature and in the presence of a roaring sea. The dark sky and wild waves press against the shoreline in an intense evocation of the moment. So, for all its gestural power the painting remains a sublime and direct response to the irresistible force of nature.

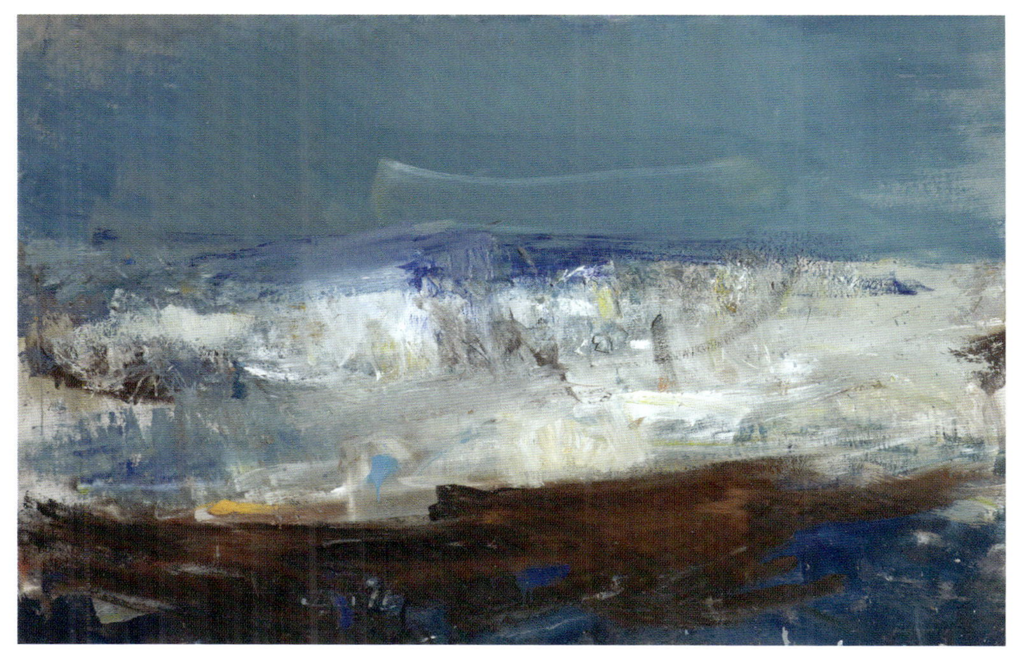

Joan Eardley, *Summer Sea*

ESME GORDON, *Leeds Permanent Building Society, new branch office, Dundee*

The 1960s, when Joan Eardley was eventually recognized as a full member of the academy, was an outstanding period of change that touched every dimension of society. The changes were social, political, and cultural, and they surely encouraged an increased democratization in cultural life, a sense of generational realignment, and a greater desire for experiment in every aspect of the arts. Most of this touched the academy.

Certainly the architecture of the period looked to reflect a modernist style while simultaneously providing mass housing and contemporary living standards. Perhaps the most recognized architect of the period, Sir Basil Spence, was never elected RSA despite his landmark works including the Scottish Pavilion at the Glasgow International Exhibition in 1938, and the redevelopment of the Gorbals area of Glasgow in the 1960s (Spence was elected ARSA in 1952, but never given full membership for he was resident in England). But those who would recognize the values of modernist architecture certainly became key figures in the academy and none more so than Esme Gordon (1910–1993). Gordon, a near contemporary of Spence, had worked with the more esteemed architect, under Thomas Tait, in the designs for the Scottish Pavilion. Gordon's architectural practice, in Edinburgh, was modest and he tended to focus on the refurbishment of churches and on business offices. Hence, following his election to the academy in 1967 he would submit his drawing and

plan for the *Leeds Permanent Building Society, Dundee* as his diploma work. If this is not the most ambitious example of urban architectural design it does reflect the restrained modernism – clean lines and solid geometries – that typified the period.

Gordon's landmark achievement, however, was in his role as Secretary to the Academy beginning in 1973. It was he who would write the first institutional history of the academy, published in 1976 as 'The Royal Scottish Academy 1826–1976'. This detailed work followed from his unearthing of the academy archives and his recognition of the value therein, for the material had been comprehensively ignored prior to his activity. He also (re)discovered the canonical photographs of his illustrious predecessor as Secretary, David Octavius Hill, housed in the collection of the academy. And, is credited with the discovery of a 'secret drawer' in the ceremonial academy desk wherein some lost architectural drawings by Thomas Hamilton were revealed; these showing neo-classical additions designed for the Royal Institution, now the academy building.

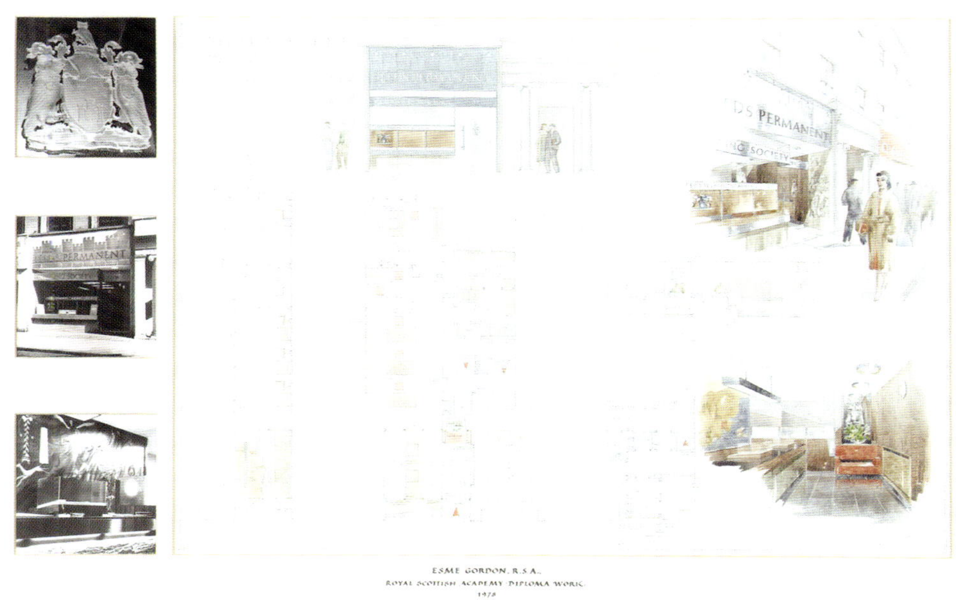

Esme Gordon, *Leeds Permanent Building Society, new branch office, Dundee*

It is certain that one of the most significant changes inaugurated by the social revolution of the 1960s was the realignment of gender relations at every level of society. Whereas Phyllis Bone, Anne Redpath and Joan Eardley had been lonely pioneers, as women entering the masculine halls of the academy from the 1940s to the early 1960s, a trickle of women academicians would become something of a stream by the 1970s, and beyond. The output of these artists could be as varied as that of their male colleagues and equally traversed a terrain from the decorative to the challenging.

Bet Low (1924–2007) was firmly rooted in the social and political nexus of the Glasgow art world. Having trained at Glasgow School of Art in the war years she exhibited with the 'Clyde Group' from 1946. Here, with her future husband, Tom Macdonald, she would be committed to a leftist programme that would situate the role of art within a social realist paradigm and so recognise working-class life as a suitable subject for painting. Later, Low would develop into a painter of austere landscapes and so her diploma presentation, following her election to the academy in 1974, is *Green Place*. Glasgow, famously and often ironically, is noted as a place-name coming from the Gaelic and loosely translated as 'dear green place'. Low, who was, in the 1950s, championed by the 'anti-academic' colourist John Duncan Fergusson and his 'Independent Group' in Glasgow, would doubtless recognise the humour in presenting this subtle allusion to the academy in Edinburgh.

In contrast Frances Walker (b.1930) though having trained in Edinburgh under William Gillies was, from the early 1950s, committed to painting in the Western Isles and would seal her links to the north of Scotland by taking a teaching post at Gray's School of Art, in Aberdeen, in 1958. Walker was elected as an associate member of the academy in 1970 and she would become a full academician in 1983. Her diploma submission was a remarkable landscape titled *Foreshore at Footdee*. Her dedication to landscape painting, and a profound 'sense of place', is evidenced in the many remarkable images she has created of Scotland's capricious geography. *Foreshore at Footdee* reflects on the marginal land between sea and shore at Footdee, in the east of Aberdeen. The foreground consists of a constructed sea defence; an arrangement of rocks and boulders designed as a 'rock armour' to absorb the energy of the waves and so save the coastline from erosion. Painted in pastel pinks, mauves and light greys to reflect the washed and weathered stones it reveals a cool and abstract sweep of land. This is complemented by the industrial buildings in the far distance and the long arc of the bay where the grey sea falls on the land. An echo of Gillies' oeuvre is evident here, but one that eschews the painterly qualities of the Edinburgh School. This is a study in texture, pattern, and abstract relations that evokes the soft calm of a summer day.

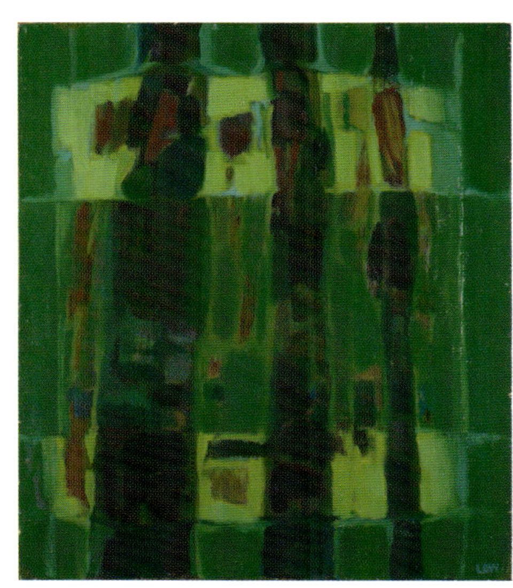

Bet Low, *Green Place*

Frances Walker, *Foreshore at Footdee*

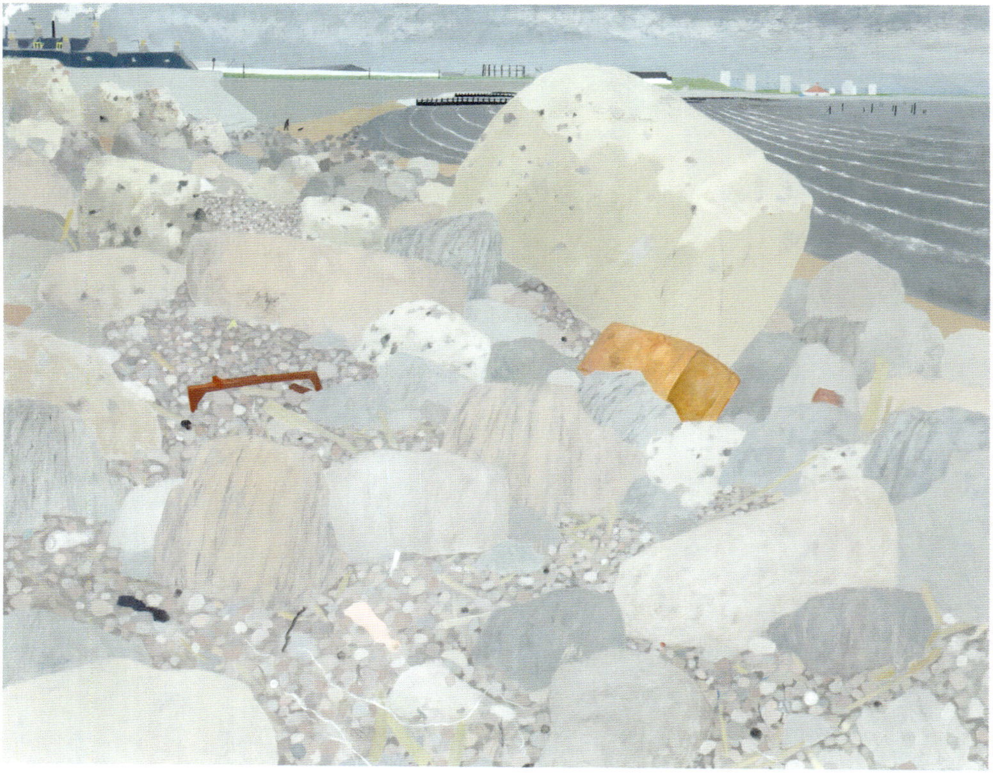

WILLIAM BROTHERSTON, *Hat (Hat for Joseph Beuys)*

The tumult and reorientations generated in the 1960s also opened out a host of new opportunities for Scottish artists. Indeed the presence of an international and experimental art became a feature of the cultural scene; especially in Edinburgh, and particularly in the period around the Edinburgh International Festival of the Arts that took place in the city every August from 1947. The academy would contribute to this febrile activity hosting exhibitions of significant modern artists ranging from Kandinsky in 1960 to Picasso in 1968; and by way of Soutine, Rouault and the American Abstract Expressionist School, amongst others, in the years between.

Meanwhile, smaller and experimental venues throughout the city would explore 'happenings', performance art, auto-destructive events, and every variety of intermedia exhibition. The apotheosis of this experimentalism was the 'Strategy Get Arts' exhibition, organized by Richard Demarco (HRSA 2001), and held at Edinburgh College of Art in the summer of 1970. Here, the cream of the German avant-garde – notably the Dusseldorf School – were invited to stage events, performances and installations that would herald the era of neo-dada art and culture. Amongst exhibiters there was Klaus Rinke, Blinky Palermo, Bernd and Hilla Becher, Sigmar Polke, Gerhard Richter and Daniel Spoerri, but the most influential figure, in terms of Scottish art, was Joseph Beuys. Beuys would present his installation *The Pack* as a centrepiece to this exhibition but he would subsequently return to Scotland,

many times, where his performances and events would make him a cult figure amongst local artists. Indeed, his trademark gilet and homburg hat came to signify the arrival of an imaginative and 'contemporary' spirit in the Scottish art world.

Richard Demarco challenged Scottish artists to respond to Beuys' intervention and William Brotherston (b.1943) would, on his election as an academician in 2005, present the sculpture *Hat* as his diploma piece. The work has a double life for when it was originally exhibited, in the Demarco Gallery, it was titled *Hat for Joseph Beuys* but it was first created as a more intimate work referencing the hat of the artists' father. Brotherston originally made the work in clay and included leaves and twigs in the mould, and these are evidenced in the finished bronze sculpture. In this respect it might be argued that the hat also references Beuys' concern with ecological issues, but these links are tenuous for the piece stands as an independent sculptural object replete with associations and meanings that are nuanced and subjective.

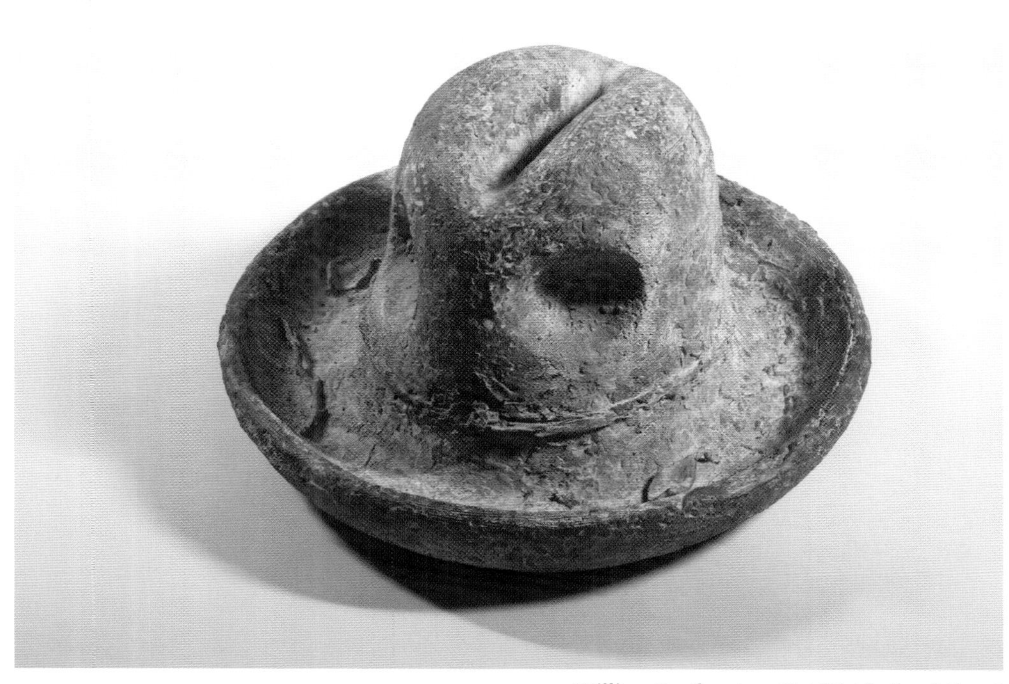

William Brotherston, *Hat (Hat for Joseph Beuys)*

ELIZABETH BLACKADDER, *Self Portrait with Cat*

JOHN HOUSTON, *Towards Skye*

DAVID MICHIE, *On the Ramblas*

For all these developments and changes, outside and sometimes within the academy, a core group of Edinburgh painters remained the most active and engaged participants in the institution. Certainly the closing decades of the 20th century saw a network of associated artists whose work was directed towards a vivid and exciting *belle peinture* approach that explored domestic subjects and landscapes.

Elizabeth Blackadder (b.1931) was a pupil of William Gillies at Edinburgh College of Art and subsequently taught in the college. Her work has been celebrated for its subtle design and complex manipulation of space. Influenced by Japanese art she has a special sensitivity for still-life and has focused on domestic objects, flowers and cats in a manner that accents the nuance of composition and spatial complexity on a two-dimensional surface. For all this, following her election to the academy in 1972, she submitted a rare self-portrait as her diploma piece, *Self Portrait with Cat*. Viewed in profile, in a mirror, and with the signature cat motif looking out at the viewer the image is a kind of statement of her mission as artist.

Blackadder's husband, John Houston (1930–2008), was likewise an Edinburgh-trained painter and elected an academician in the same year as his wife, contributing a landscape view of Skye as his diploma work. *Towards Skye* is typical of Houston's landscape painting in its bold and expressive brushwork. It is untypical in its muted colour scheme, based on tones of grey, for Houston was an extraordinary colourist. He had been much influenced by the long memory of Edvard Munch's exhibition, held at the Society of Scottish Artists in 1931, and a show that shaped the painting of his tutors in Edinburgh and generations of Scottish artists. Houston explored the expressionism of Munch's late work and recognised its echo in the painting of the German school, this would reverberate in his own expressionism and soulful representation of nature.

The work of David Michie (b.1928) has, equally, demonstrated a decorative panache and general *joie de vivre* that exemplifies the vibrancy and allure of Edinburgh painting. Elected to the academy in 1972 his diploma submission *On the Ramblas* displays the vivid colour and visual spectacle that might be anticipated from the son of Anne Redpath. Yet this image is remarkable not simply for the delight of its pattern and decorative effect. Visiting the radical city of Barcelona, in Spain, just at the end of Franco's fascist dictatorship Michie recognised the contrast between the energy and vivacity of life on La Rambla and the threatening shadow of an ever-present political repression. The two symbolic figures in the painting represent this duality, and are set against the effervescence and verve of the principal thoroughfare in the Catalan capital.

Elizabeth Blackadder, *Self Portrait with Cat*

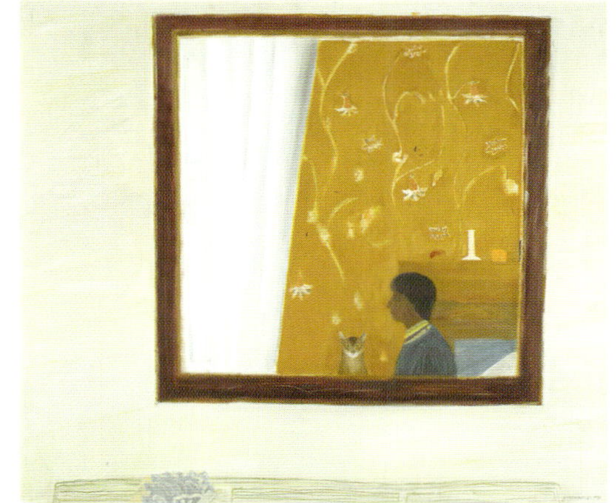

John Houston, *Towards Skye*

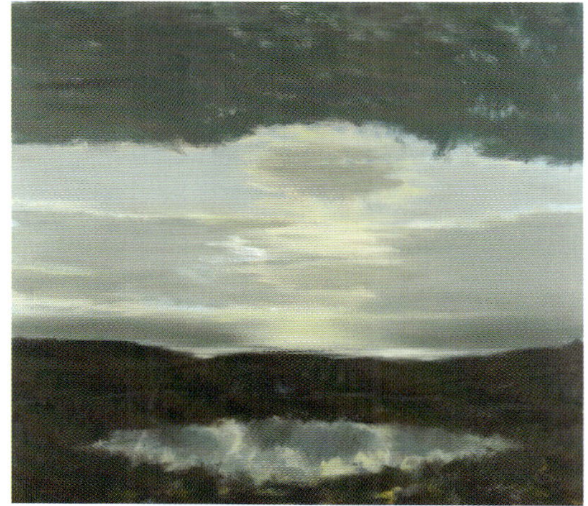

David Michie, *On the Ramblas*

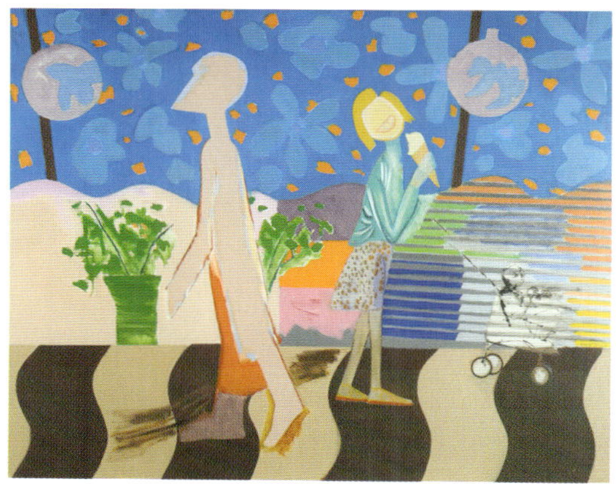

JAMES CUMMING, *Table Assembly with Rusted Tins*

If the academy was something of a social and cultural network in this period it did reach beyond the grid of the New Town salons and the convention of virtuoso painting.

James Cumming (1922–1991) was born north of the River Forth, in Dunfermline, and, though he studied at Edinburgh College of Art, he eschewed the pathway that was most usually taken by his mentors and peers. It was commonplace, amongst the Edinburgh School, to complete their artistic education with residences in France and in Italy; most often in the studio of Andre L'hote in Paris. When Cumming completed his education he undertook a travelling scholarship and chose to spend this period on the Isle of Lewis. This was in the year 1949–50 and the western isles were marginal to post-war developments in Europe and London, and indeed in Edinburgh. Here, however, Cumming saw something of an authenticity and integrity in the world of crofters and their communities. His painting, for all its modernism, drew inspiration from the rocky landscape, the wild sea, the folklore, and most particularly the people of the Hebrides. These were certainly his finest works, and, as Joanna Soden has recognised 'For nearly two decades Cumming's experiences of Lewis furnished his paintings (Macdonald, et.al. 26).

Cumming's style was inflected with cubist fragmentation and often described fractured monumental figures, but the quality of painted surface and composi-

tional complexity was remarkable. Following his election as an academician in 1970 he submitted *Table Assembly with Rusted Tins* as his diploma piece. If this is not one of his epic Lewis works it is nevertheless characteristic of the sophisti-cated structure and arrangement he brought to his compositions. A still life, not of flowers and refined domestic ornaments but of 'rusted tins', it echoes the vernacular concerns of his most distinctive painting. The table-top pushed upwards towards the picture plane accents the two-dimensional nature of the painting, while the assembly of tins and objects creates an abstract pattern that connotes the best of 'synthetic' cubism in its various manifestations throughout the European canon. The sense of colour, too, is muted and subtle and seems to react against the flamboyance of Edinburgh painting. In this way it might be argued that the focus, and variety, of academic painting in the post-war period opened out from an expressionist to a constructivist dynamic.

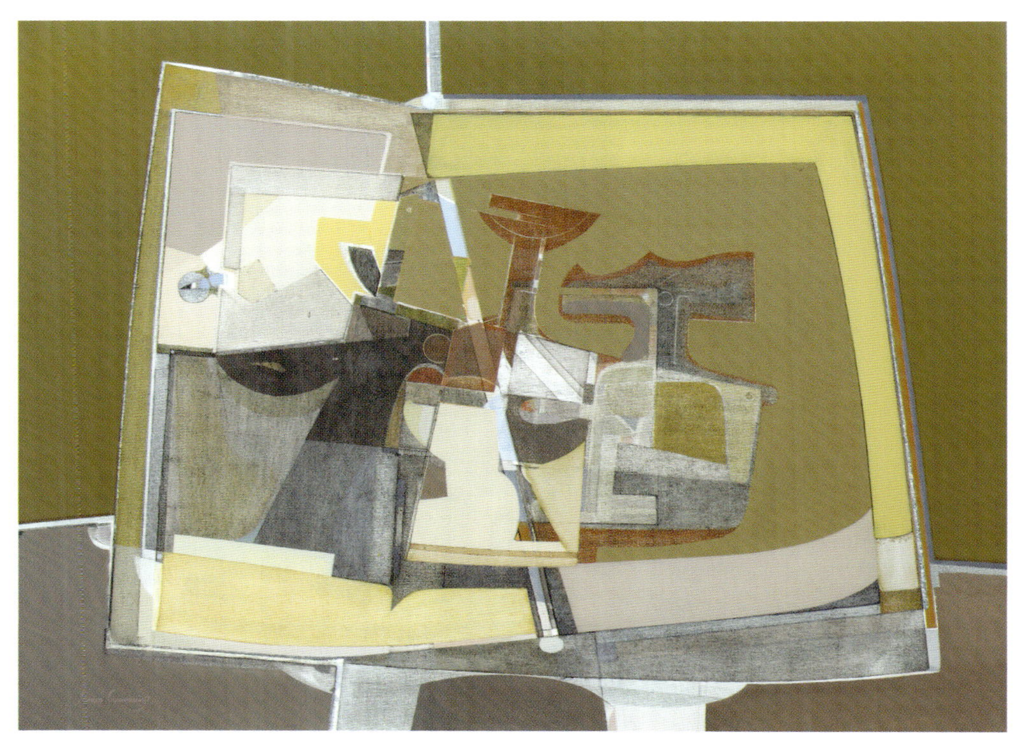

James Cumming, *Table Assembly with Rusted Tins*

JACK KNOX, *Snack in a Dutch Museum*

The example of James Cumming's 'difference' was repeated in academic elections throughout the 1970s. Jack Knox (b.1936) was elected to the academy in 1979 but had trained in Glasgow School of Art and taught for the greater part of his career in Duncan of Jordanstone College of Art in Dundee. The trajectory of Knox's work was typical of those Scottish artists who were alert to international developments in the decades of the 1960s and 1970s. Initially fascinated by the experiments of the Abstract Expressionists in the United States, he later came to explore the 'counter-culture' of Pop Art. Where the interest in Pop Art came to accent a fascination with the 'everyday' in Knox's work, and particularly with the unique qualities of ordinary objects, a visit to the Rijksmuseum in Amsterdam, during 1972, led to an intrigue with 17th century Dutch still-life painting. Here the sense of each familiar object as precious and freighted with meaning came to be reflected in his painting. But, still employing the cool and detached 'Pop' manner in his painting the effect became one of sardonic and slightly amused indifference.

The diploma work *Snack in a Dutch Museum* might be understood in this light. A stairwell, graphically described; a tiled wall, ironically echoing the 'grid' of academic painting but with each tile 'expressively' painted; the bannisters and stair-rails, modern and tubular in the manner of Bauhaus ornament; and, crisply painted on the right of the composition, the 'snack'. This last is the core of the still life, a glass of beer, a hamburger and a bread-roll are perched on a block-like balustrade. These objects, separated from the rest of the work by virtue of their colour and finish, are meticulously painted and so imbued with a near religious character. They are, at once, familiar, ordinary, distinctive, disconnected, mysterious and ironic.

The seemingly disinterested qualities in works by Cumming and by Knox point to an analytical component within academic art in Scotland. This quasi-philosophical element reached back to the character of academic art in the 19th century and before that to the sensibility of the Scottish Enlightenment. It is appropriate to acknowledge that the story of modern Scottish art was not exclusively expressionist and colourist but contained, also, the grain of a challenging intellectualism. Cumming, Knox, and others, have been examples of this trope and from within the academy structure.

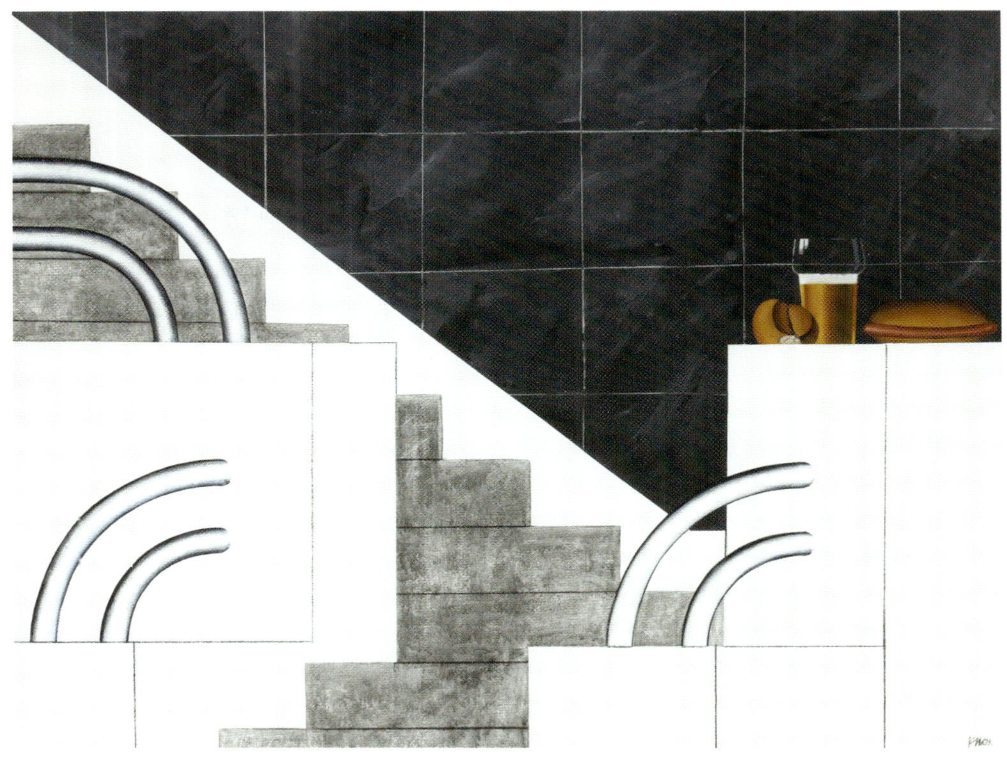

Jack Knox, *Snack in a Dutch Museum*

BILL SCOTT, *Twentieth Century Pad*

An important example of this intellectualism is evidenced in the work of the first sculptor ever to be elected President of the Royal Scottish Academy. Bill Scott (1935–2012) was first elected to the academy in 1984 and was to become President in 2007, a post he held until his death in 2012. An eminent sculptor of long standing he taught at Edinburgh College of Art, was Chair of the Edinburgh Sculpture Workshop, and was a key figure in the dissemination and development of Scottish sculpture on the international stage.

Scott's practice described an arc across the various categories of modern sculpture; chiefly working in constructed motifs he also would carve materials and would model works to be cast in bronze. The dynamic of his practice was a concern with personal and social space, and this made him an archetype for the academy itself. For, like the painter he was concerned with the complex representation of space, and, like the architect he was fascinated by the ways in which individuals occupy space. So, the rationale of his sculpture was a perfect fit for the many genres of the academy.

His diploma work, *Twentieth Century Pad*, is a cast bronze that exemplifies his core subject. An abstract figure, in an open room, stands close to what may be a stairwell, or what may be an end wall, and is in relation to various forms and objects. There is an austere surrealism to the work and it contains an understated theatricality. Sculpturally it is intimate rather than monumental and it speaks to a human scale. Interestingly Scott, as a student in the 1950s, is known to have been influenced by Ann Henderson (RSA 1976) and her diploma work *Woman and Chair* is an equally intimate and intriguing bronze. Scott's work, however, is the more engrossing for it conjures with levels of thought and association that remain intellectually abstruse. This disturbance and ambiguity is the work's greatest strength and speaks to its continuing fascination.

The writer of Bill Scott's obituary, the fellow sculptor William Brotherston, has noted that 'he (Scott) assumed office at a time of change' and that he oversaw, as President of the academy, a number of changes designed to make the academy relevant to the contemporary period in the development of art. These, including the redesignation of the annual student exhibition as 'New Contemporaries' and the international expansion of the academy's associations and roles, will be a lasting testament to Bill Scott, but the body of his sculpture will remain a worthy and respected memorial.

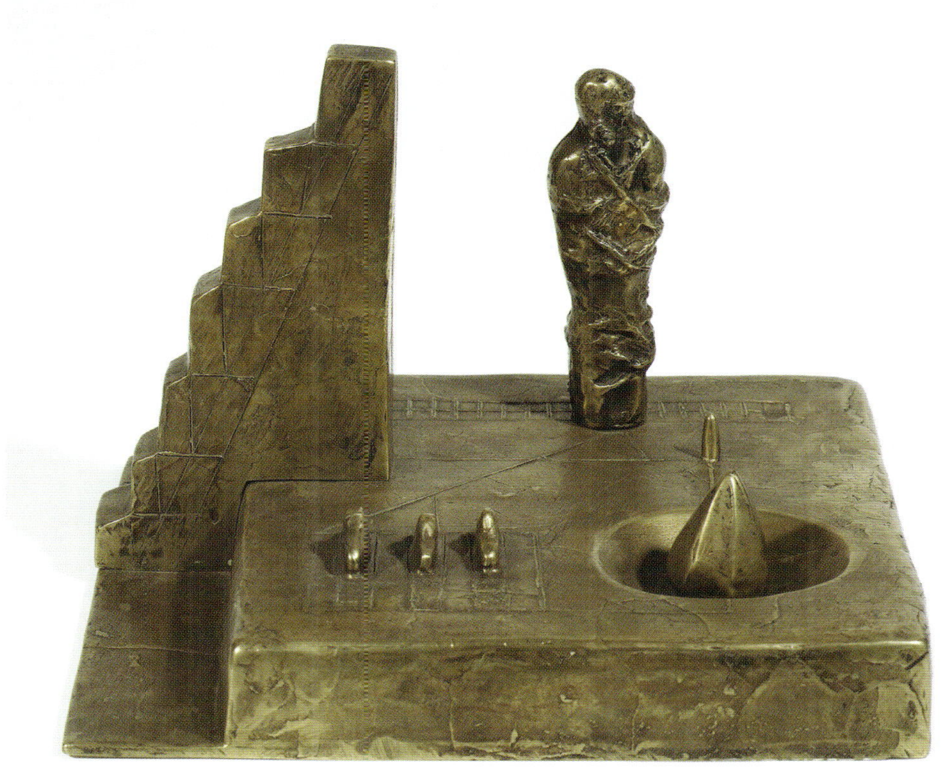

Bill Scott, *Twentieth Century Pad*

ISI METZSTEIN, *College at Cumbernauld*

Bill Scott's concern with space and the ways in which human beings inhabited the spaces around them was a sculptural concern. But it had clear parallels with architecture and was, perhaps, the key coordinate in a modernist architecture; especially as this had been theorised in Le Corbusier's modernist vision. The heir to Corbusier's vision, in Scotland, was surely Isi Metzstein (1928–2012) who became a full academician in 1999 having deposited his *College at Cumbernauld* in the diploma collection.

As an individual Metzstein found himself at the crossroads of European history in the 20th century. Born in Berlin to Polish Jewish parents he lost his father at a young age and, brought up by his mother, he would escape Germany on the Kindertransport following the events of Kristallnacht in November 1938. Brought to Clydebank at the age of ten he was, by the age of 17, an apprentice in the architectural firm of Gillespie, Kidd and Coia. In the post war period he attended – in the evening – architectural classes at Glasgow School of Art where he met his lifelong collaborator Andy MacMillan. Under the auspices of Gillespie, Kidd and Coia this partnership would be responsible for some of the finest modernist buildings in Scotland. The firm of Gillespie, Kidd and Coia was principally associated with the design of chapels for the Roman Catholic church and Metzstein and MacMillan's first great success was St Paul's in the new town of Glenrothes. Completed in 1957 this was an ambitious modernist design that fundamentally challenged the traditional forms of church architecture and set in motion a radical reassessment of chapel design. There followed a range of new designs for churches that lit-up the landscape of Scotland's new towns, and beyond. The masterpiece, however, was surely the St Peter's Seminary at Cardross in Argyll and Bute. Completed in 1966 this was recognised as a building of international significance and an exemplary expression of Corbusier's method and theory. Designed as a seminary for the training of priests it fell victim to a change in church policy where priests were allocated to training within the community. It now lies in ruins and remains the subject of much debate amongst the Scottish intelligentsia and conservationists.

Unusually Metzstein, who would also serve as Treasurer to the Academy, submitted a secular piece for this diploma work. This is his design for a *College at Cumbernauld*. Gillespie, Kidd and Coia were given the original commission for the design of Cumbernauld Technical College in the mid-1970s and the building, now, has been subject to further accretions and development. Metzstein's design, however, gives evidence of his creative imagination and modernist vision: a light and airy structure, all cantilevered forms and balanced platforms, and complete with continuous ribbon fenestration. In many ways the vision of Metzstein and MacMillan continued that astonishing Glasgow tradition of creating adventurous and fascinating architectural schemes, fully attuned to developments on the continent of Europe.

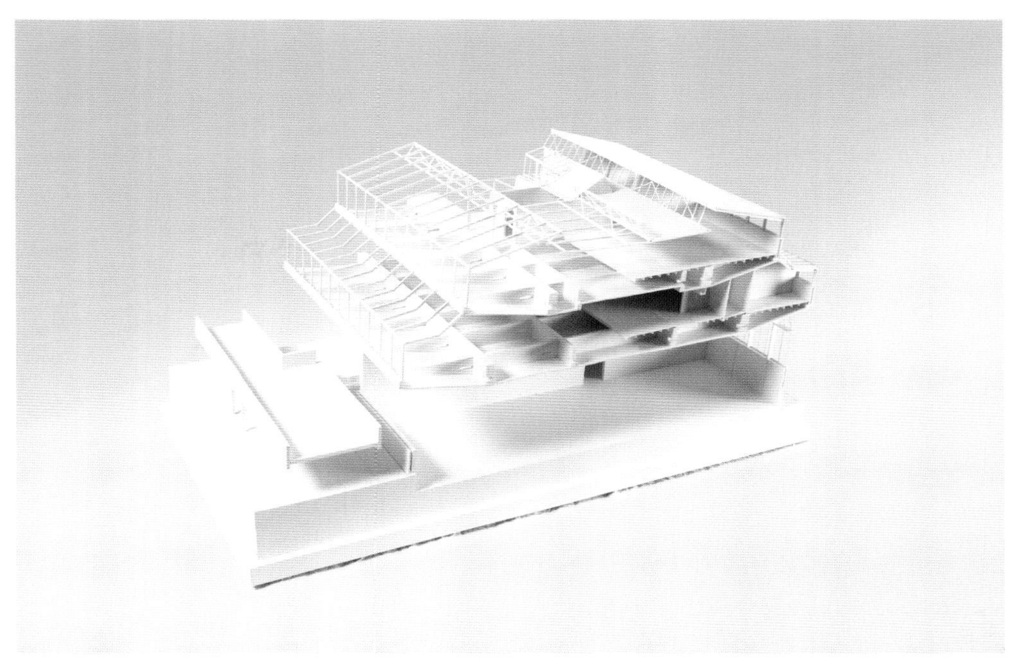

Isi Metzstein, *College at Cumbernauld*

WILL MACLEAN, *Boston 'T'*

During the 1990s the academy grew in a manner that was both progressive and expansive. Moreover, as Scottish art widened its horizons the dominance of Edinburgh painters was fractured. Will Maclean (b.1941) had trained at Gray's School of Art in Aberdeen and his northern sensibility informed the nature and content of his art.

Maclean comes from a Highland background and so his work is shaped by the memory and poetry of Gaelic culture. His subjects range from the history of the Highland Clearances, through the spirit world of Gaelic mythology and storytelling, and into the sense of enforced emigration and diaspora. His work has primarily been completed in shallow box constructions replete with crafted and found objects. These boxes display an imagined world that connotes the intricate and spectral realms of a shadow culture; a place of fragile memory and enigmatic symbol. Most often the boxes are worked and worn so that they appear weathered, perhaps salt-sprayed, and the effect is one of looking through a window into a mysterious, disconcerting and half-remembered netherworld.

Given the history of the Highlands and the Gael – a history of a disrupted culture and community, a displaced feudal and crofting society, a marginalised seafaring group destined to emigration – it is unsurprising that Maclean should also reflect upon the idea of diaspora.
His election to the academy in 1991 was marked by the submission of *Boston 'T'* as his diploma work. The work was completed following a research trip to the eastern seaboard of the United States, a trip that was financed by a Gillies Travel Award from the academy. Here, Maclean surveyed the maritime museums of Nantucket, Boston and Mystic Seaport. *Boston 'T'* contains the memory of that visit replete with the symbolic notes of the seafaring communities, the whaling industry and the related museum artefacts. The 'T' shape that forms the basis of the construction is a formal compositional device but also recalls the tram system in Boston; known locally as the Boston 'T'. The recessed figures, sailing ships and symbols provide vignettes that connote individual memories from the various museums and their collections. While the painted and rubbed surface of the box construction recollects the mood of sea and sky that is the abiding motif of maritime life and culture.

These memories of fading cultures and civilisations, these recollections of marginal communities and seafaring adventurers, are the leitmotifs of a sensibility attuned to a dimension of Scottish history and life that has often been lost in the privilege afforded to activities in the 'central belt' of the nation. Maclean has created from these 'fringes' and 'peripheries' an internationally recognised art that speaks to core human values and substantial symbolic meaning.

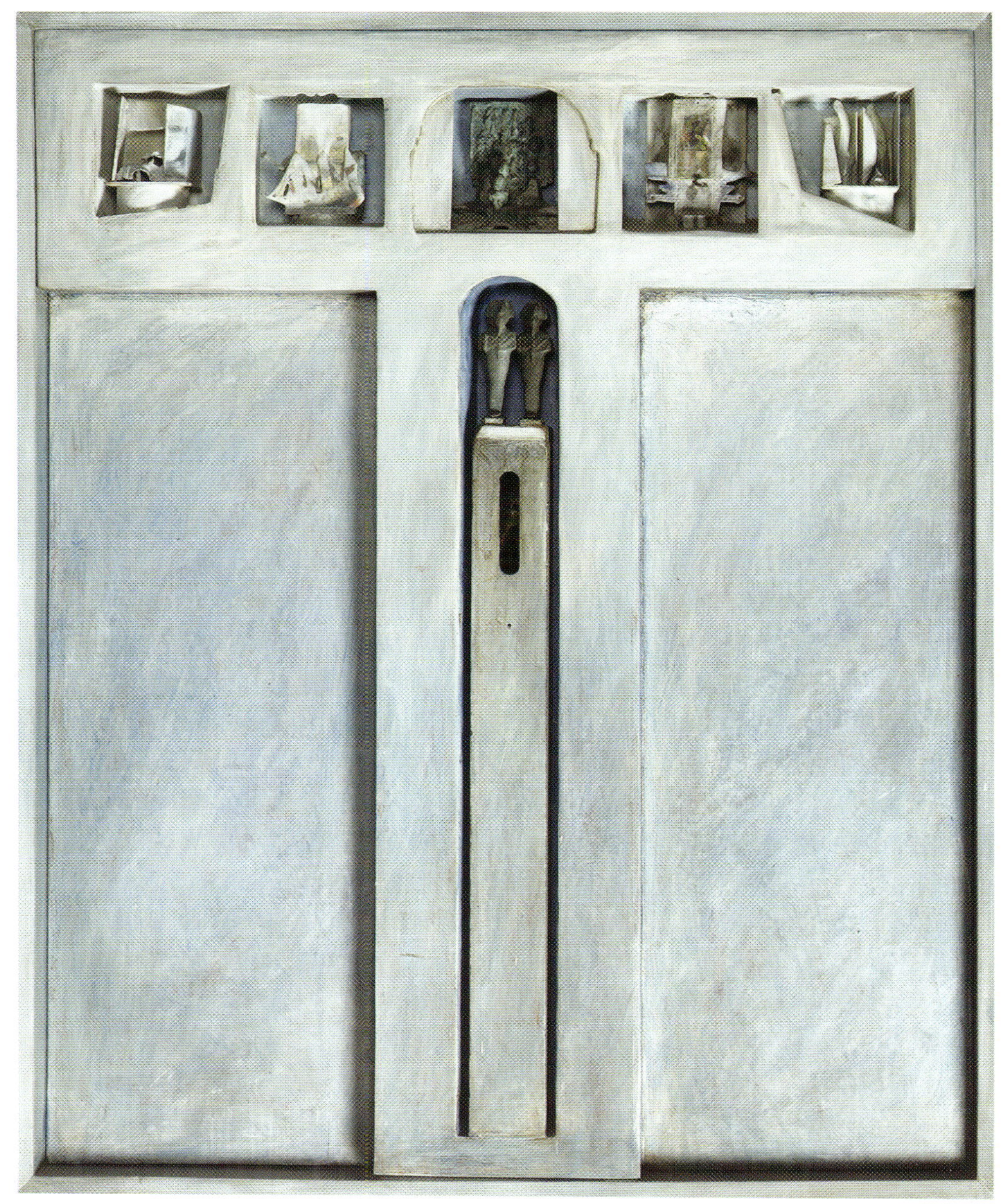

Will Maclean, *Boston 'T'*

JOYCE CAIRNS, *Polish Journey*

The concern with history, complex cultural identities, and the relationship between the individual and society would become a characteristic of Scottish art from the 1980s and this was reflected within the academy. Joyce Cairns (b.1947) was elected a full academician in 1998 and chose as her diploma work a piece from her ambitious project 'War Tourist'.

The 'War Tourist' project was assisted by a Gillies Travel Award, given from the academy in 1997, though the broader concern with war had been a subject for the artist from 1984. The Gillies Award, however, allowed Cairns to journey through the war sites and the concentration camps of Europe. This journey was both historical and personal. Historical, for it permitted the artist to engage with the memory of a catastrophic world war and its long shadow. Personal, for her father was a Major in the Cameron Highlanders and the imagery is, in part, the story of his war. The narrative is, however, much larger than this for Cairns travelled through the sites, and sights, of the First World War and the Second World War, the concentration camps in Germany and Poland, the collective memories of the 'Home Front', and also recognised the contemporary resurrection of ethnic genocide in Bosnia in the early 1990s.

Her diploma work, *Polish Journey*, is a defining piece from the wider project. Painted on a large scale it contains a collage of figures, symbols, objects, and insignia that mix memory with memorial in a poignant threnody to the victims of war. The central figure is an imagined vision of the artist's younger self; here in a partial uniform and adorned by a locket in which a picture of her father is captured. Surrounding this figure the fragments of imagery that represent the remains of lost souls: the manipulated children deported to the camps, the abandoned and broken dolls viewed in concentration camp museums, the signature badges and cloths designed to stigmatise the 'enemies of the state', the canister containing 'Zyklon' gas pellets representing 'the final solution'. This is both a powerful and tragic vision that presents a dark kaleidoscope of signs and cyphers. And here the collision of history and individual consciousness is marked by the wreath of poppies, 'In Remembrance', signifying the everlasting memorial to the war dead and the particular representation of this ceremony in the artist's home village. So, history and biography are one and the sense of shared experience, a shared responsibility, become moot.

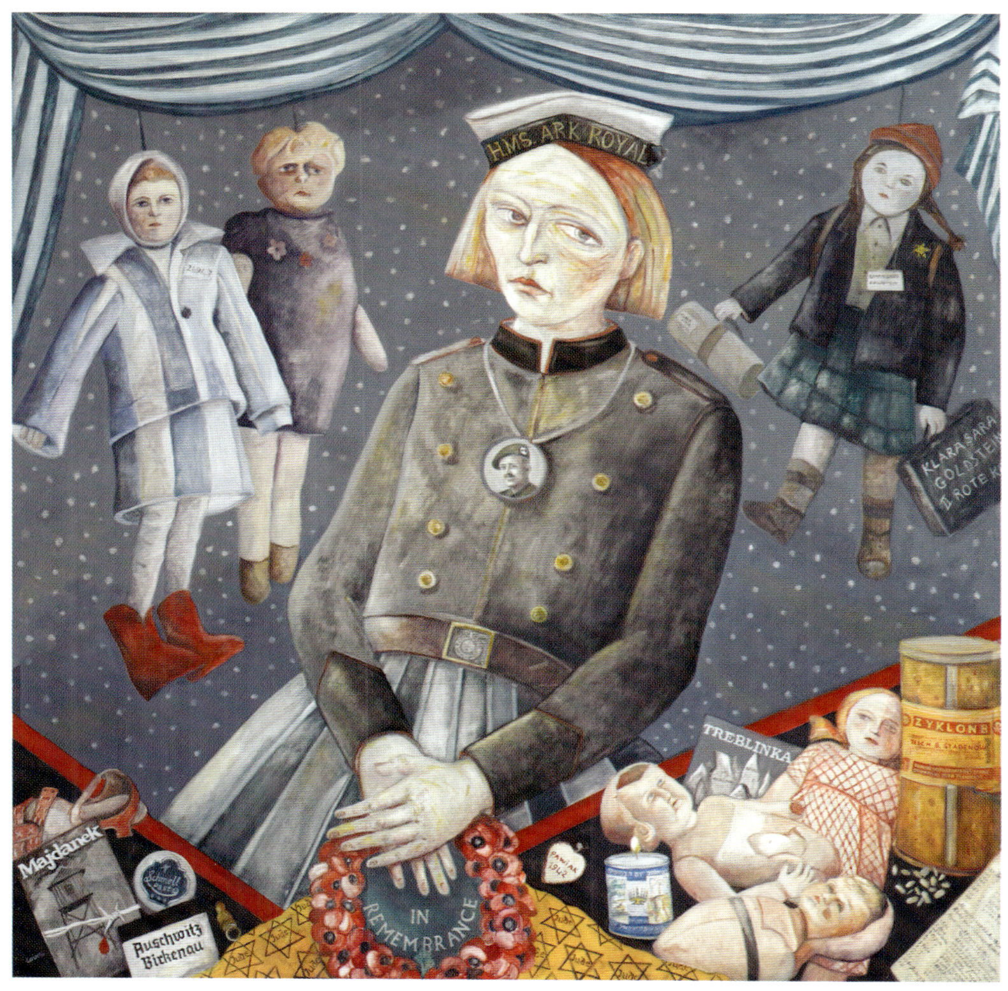

Joyce Cairns, *Polish Journey*

ALEXANDER MOFFAT, *The Rock (The Radical Road)*

Joyce Cairns' oeuvre was rooted in the return to figurative art that was a feature of Scottish art in the 1980s. This, in turn, was a fraction of the larger move towards figuration internationally; notably in Germany, Italy and in America. In Scotland much of this interest was determined by a reevaluation of German Expressionist painting of the 1930s, especially Max Beckmann, Otto Dix and Georg Grosz. The chief protagonist of this figurative revival had been Alexander Moffat, who encouraged a generation of younger painters in his role as Head of Drawing and Painting at Glasgow School of Art.

Moffat (b.1943) had been part of a radical generation, trained at Edinburgh College of Art, who fervently rejected academicism in the 1960s. With the painter John Bellany (HRSA 1987), and the writer and critic Alan Bold, he championed a social art based on the lives of the working class and shaped by a figurative aesthetic that was designed to counter the more bourgeois tastes of the academy. This extended to a series of controversial open-air exhibitions, from 1963–65, that presented a *Salon de Refuses* to the public during the period of the academy's Edinburgh Festival exhibitions.

Moffat was elected an academician in 2005 and deposited his epic *The Rock (The Radical Road)* as his diploma work. This is a powerful expressionist landscape of Salisbury Crags, the outcrop of rock that sits at the east end of Edinburgh's 'Royal Mile' in the dramatic setting of Holyrood Park. This extraordinary rock,

a counterpoint to Castle Rock at the west end of the 'Mile', is a key landmark in the city. The subtitle of the composition, 'The Radical Road', refers to the creation of a pathway on the crag mooted, as a project, by Walter Scott. The path was constructed during the 1820s. It used the labour of weavers who had been made unemployed by economic slump and who had been engaged in insurrectionist activity in the period after the French revolution; hence, 'The Radical Road'. This kind of rebellion against aristocratic power and social control was a leitmotif in Moffat's art and became a feature of his own work and that of his most talented pupils.

In 1985 Moffat would curate an exhibition of these younger figurative painters titled 'New Image Glasgow'. This exhibition, held in the Third Eye Centre in Glasgow's Sauchiehall Street, foregrounded artists who, as Moffat noted in his catalogue essay 'now present to us an emotional authenticity and a directness of expression which communicates with compelling immediacy' (Moffat 6). This would become characteristic of a renaissance of Scottish painting in the late 1980s and this 'new image' would become fully expressed in the internationally important 'blockbuster' exhibition 'The Vigorous Imagination – New Scottish Art' held in the Scottish National Gallery of Modern Art in the summer of 1987. Moffat, it might be argued, was the progenitor of this defining moment in the post-war period.

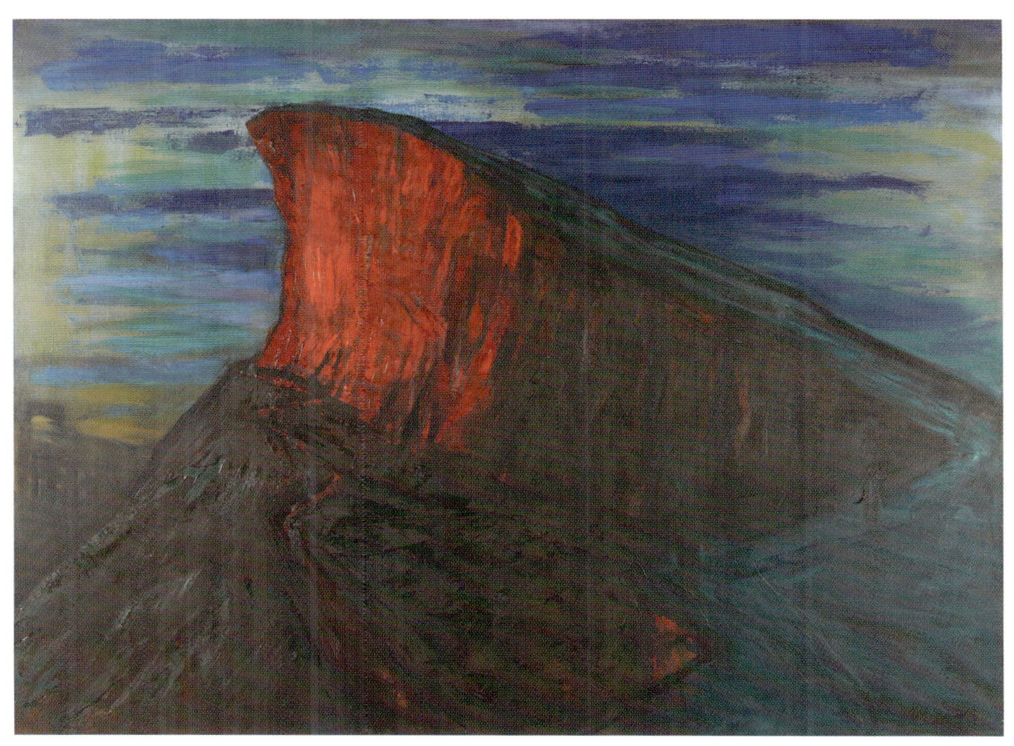

Alexander Moffat, *The Rock (The Radical Road)*

ADRIAN WISZNIEWSKI, *Sculptress*

Amongst the cohort of Alexander Moffat's students at Glasgow School of Art, and an important exhibitor in the 'New Image Glasgow' exhibition, was Adrian Wiszniewski (b.1958). The trajectories of figurative painting in Glasgow tended to describe two divergent arcs. One, following closely to Moffat's vision, was towards a social and political art and the exemplars of this, in period, were Ken Currie and Peter Howson. The other was orientated towards a fantasy art, sometimes viewed as 'postmodern' in its propensity for fractured narratives and random significations, and here Steven Campbell has been viewed as the key personality. Adrian Wiszniewski has been associated with this latter trope and it is the case that he is often freighted with Campbell. However, as a major contributor to 'The Vigorous Imagination' exhibition in 1987 Wiszniewski was noted for creating painting that contained 'a reverie of indefinite longing, of half-understood, ambivalent desires' (NGS, The Vigorous Imagination 114) and his open, associative and freely-imagined painting has embraced a creative spontaneity that chimes with automatist technique and surrealist imagining.

Wiszniewski's subject matter generally explored the figure in the landscape, or in the domestic setting, and most often gave expression to languid scenes of daydream or torpor. This was a contemporary expression of 'luxe, calme et volupte' but it could also insinuate a dissonant note into the sensual realm. Early works like *Attack of a Right-Wing Nature* conjured with Darwinian notions of determinism and allied these with negative political associations. Equally, *The Sculptor's Nightmare* presented a complex scene where the sculptor, with hammer and chisel, cuts into the body of a sleeping female. In each of these works the characteristic linear style, almost rococo in its rhythm, and the intense colour, brightly illustrative, offered a decorative quality at odds with the dark innuendo of the imagery. In later work the intensely rhythmic pattern of the painting was reduced to flat bands of colour and this is the manner of his diploma work. Having accepted election to the academy in 2005 Wiszniewski presented a small portrait-like head titled *Sculptress* as his diploma work. This work seems to parallel the earlier *The Sculptor's Nightmare* though it is more benign and passive in its nature. The work also eschews the more loaded symbolic motifs of his earlier painting and presents a simple organic object as the subject of his protagonist's muse. But the head, for all the world looking like an icon with an emblematic 'attribute', presents that dimension of Wiszniewski's practice that accents colour and line as the core components of his aesthetic.

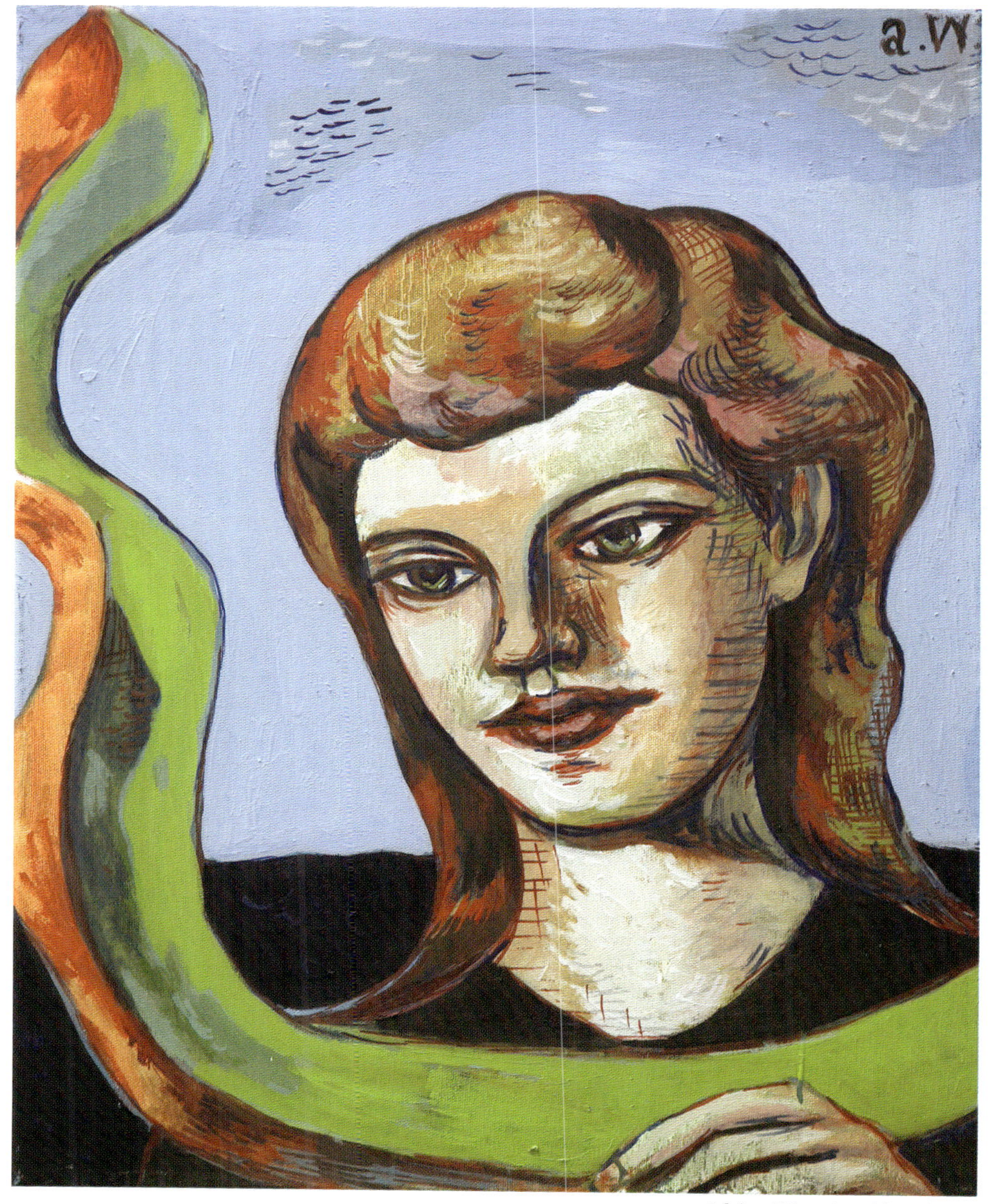

Adrian Wiszniewski, *Sculptress*

It is the case that 'The Vigorous Imagination' exhibition was a landmark in post-war painting and sculpture from Scotland, and a number of the protagonists from this exhibition are now academicians. Calum Colvin (b.1961) was elected an academician in 2004 and bears the distinction of being the first artist to be elected whose practice was photography. Certainly David Octavius Hill has been most remembered as a photographer – as part of the canonical Hill and Adamson partnership in the 1840s – but he had been elected as a painter. Evidently, Colvin's work embodies painting, and other media, but his 'product' is always a photograph. In fact Colvin's work is, typically, a constructed three-dimensional set replete with vernacular and found objects. The set is then carefully painted with a given scene, most often referencing a work of fine art. And the completed construction is then photographed in order to create the finished artwork.

His diploma piece *Venus Anadyomene (After Titian)*, is evidence of this process. Venus emerges from the sea that is, paradoxically, locked within a commonplace sitting room. The walls have been painted in order to imagine a clouded sky but the window frame and curtains are evident as are the ornaments that adorn the room; in fact her body has been painted across a profoundly utilitarian chest-of-drawers. Meanwhile, the goddess emerges naked and in characteristic pose wrings out her hair.

This melding of the mythic and the colloquial, the epic and the ordinary, is typical of Colvin's subtle and intelligent work. In fact this diploma piece is taken from a larger project titled 'Sacred and Profane'. In 1998 Colvin was invited, by the National Galleries of Scotland, to select and 're-imagine' works from their collection. Alongside works by Canova and Rubens he selected Titian's *Venus Anadyomene*, from c.1520. This 'sacred' image he re-worked in the 'profane' medium of photography and so recognised the multi-layered irony of his aesthetic and practice.

In context Colvin was amongst that group of Scottish artists from the 1980s and 1990s who produced a disruptive and challenging art rooted in a post-modern disposition. That is, he explored open narratives that were subject to infinite interpretation. Moreover he recognised, and challenged, the hegemony of the Western canon and constantly explored issues of authority, identity, power, 'truth', national discourse and global theory that recognised the multiplicity and variety of viewpoints in a complex multicultural world. *Venus Anadyomene (After Titian)* is one dimension of that critical perception, and one that interrogates the nature of the Western canon in fine art; in this sense it is a fascinating intervention in academic practice.

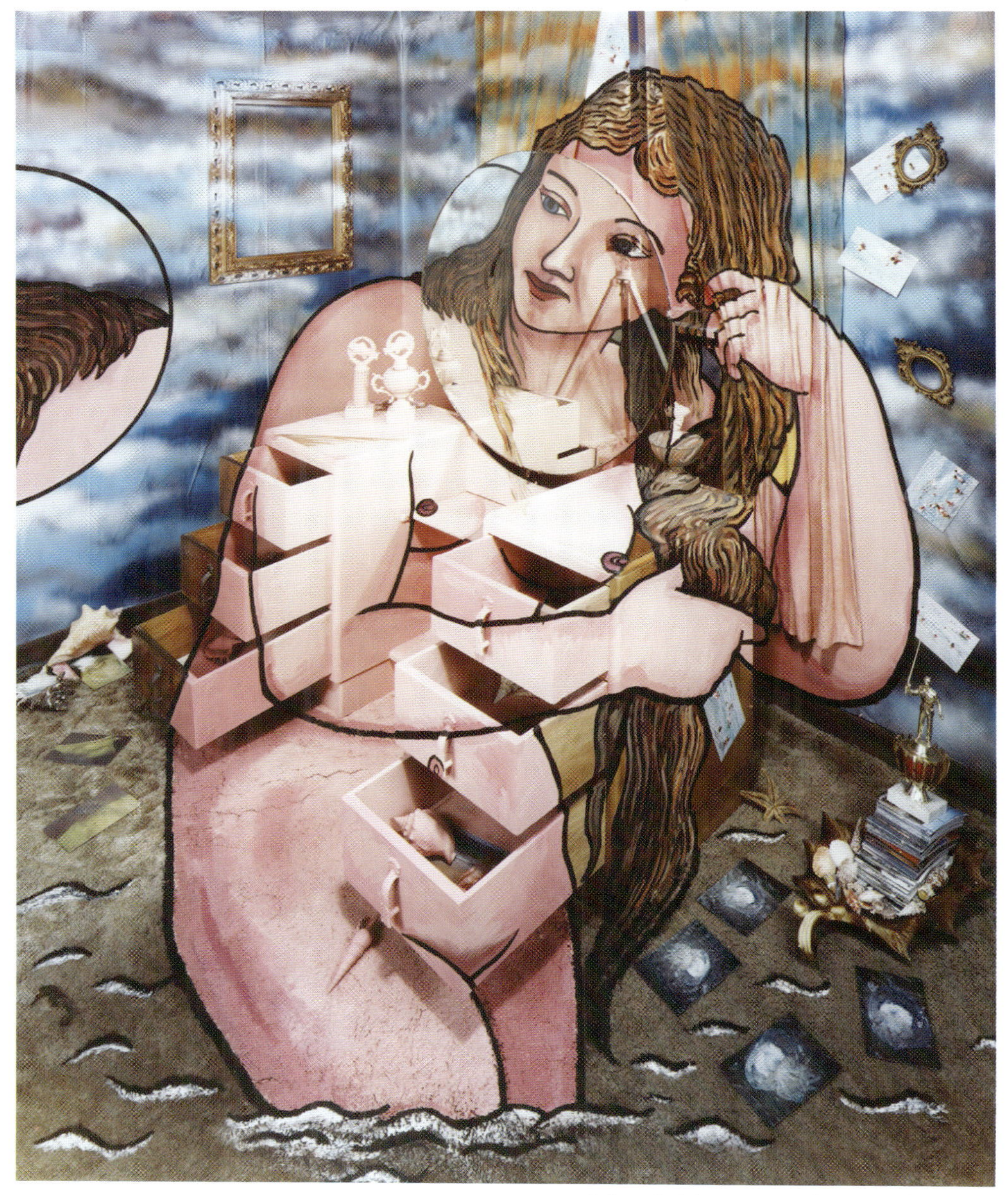

Calum Colvin, *Venus Anadyomene (After Titian)*

KATE WHITEFORD, *From the Red Cabinet*

Whereas the impetus for 'The Vigorous Imagination' exhibition had been the renaissance of figurative art in Scotland – and both Wiszniewski and Colvin were vital to that moment – a counterpoint was presented, within the rooms of the Scottish National Gallery of Modern Art, in the work of Kate Whiteford. Whiteford (b.1952) created an extraordinary quasi-abstract installation as her contribution to the exhibition. Here, the walls were painted an intense red and inscribed with black stripes. These lines, horizontal and vertical on contrasting walls, were hand-drawn and so each was distinctive and fractured. Moreover, through the thickening and narrowing of the lines, they created a rhythm or tempo and seemed to measure time in a manner that was almost musical. Whiteford overlaid her horizontal stripes with a wave motif that further enhanced the rhythmical component in the installation. Even more subtly the red and black lines created a polarity of positive and negative perception such that the sense of presence and absence was palpable. This dark and indeed mysterious space was quite unlike anything else in 'The Vigorous Imagination' exhibition. It was quiet and meditative, and a kind of 'cave of shadows'; in fact an evocative ambient experience.

This approach to image making was indicative of Whiteford's art and thought-world. An interest in deep and hidden history led to a fascination with the procedures of the archaeological dig, and the sense of layering and uncovering passages of time. Whiteford recognised that these layers of history were always esoteric and contingent and so represented this concept as a kind of ideogram; a world expressed through discrete symbols, and even moods. Most often these images would focus on classical antiquity, or indeed upon Pictish symbols. Alternatively they might be written into the landscape itself and echo an object of local association, such as the magnificent landwork *Shadow of a Necklace* at Mount Stuart on the Isle of Bute. But Whiteford has also been sensitive to the re-presentation of antiquarian objects in cabinets; either in the ubiquitous museum cabinet or in the more arcane 'cabinet of curiosities'. Consequently her diploma work, following her election to the academy in 2006, was a pair of watercolour images titled *From the Red Cabinet*. The cabinet motif had previously appeared in an installation for Agnew's, London, in 2001, but the sense of a 'cabinet' or room that displays a range of obscure and cryptic objects was a feature of Renaissance Europe and a prized display for monarchs and connoisseurs alike. Whiteford's interest remains in the arcane nature of these objects and the near occult nature of their semiotics. Her diploma piece, then, is a kind of testimony to her highly original and fascinating vision.

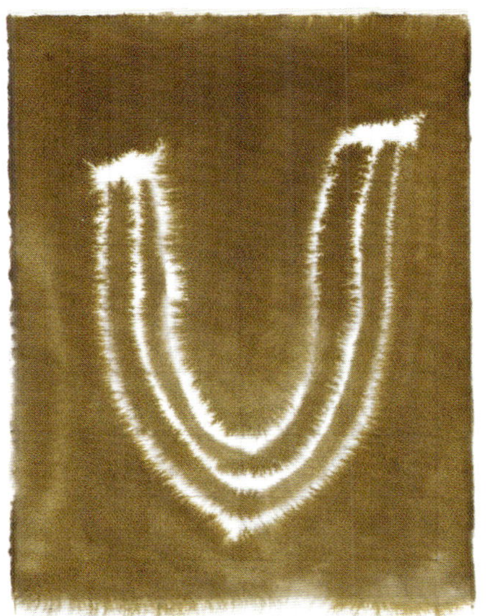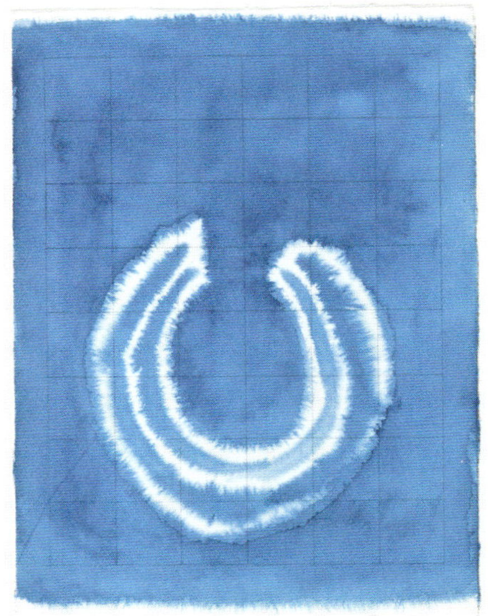

Kate Whiteford, *From the Red Cabinet* (diptych)

MARIAN LEVEN, *Weathering*

The evocation of mood and the sense of mystery that can be seen in the work of Kate Whiteford has an echo elsewhere amongst recent artists elected to the roll of academicians. Marian Leven (b.1944) is a native of Fife but chose to go to Gray's School of Art in Aberdeen in order that she might re-connect with her Highland ancestry and with the culture of the Gael. Much of her early painting was rooted in landscape, and indeed on the arbitrary and capricious nature of weather systems within the Scottish landscape. In this sense her work chimes with a tradition of academic painting that goes back to the 19th century. Examples are legion but would include J. Francis Williams' (RSA 1829) *Scene on the Ayrshire Coast – Storm Clouds*, Horatio McCulloch's (RSA 1838) *Landscape, Evening*, Robert B. Nisbet's (RSA 1902) *Landscape with Hail Cloud*, Joseph M. Henderson's (RSA 1935) *Summer Clouds*, and on to the contemporary period.

In the years after 2002 Leven's painting moved from a quasi-abstract landscape painting that evoked a sense of place to a fascination with the atmospherics of weather and nature. This coincided with a period as artist-in-residence at Sabhal Mòr Ostaig, the Gaelic College in Skye. Leven was, in fact, the first artist to be honoured with this position and here her work developed landscape imagery towards a nuanced and abstract 'weatherscape'. Consequently she worked less in nature and more in the studio, and increasingly the plastic nature of the 'mark' became an important feature of her painting. This shift from the denotive to the connotive began to represent the 'landscape' as a kind of minimal abstraction and so, following her election as an academician in 2004, Leven submitted the painting *Weathering* as her diploma work.

Weathering is interesting for its abstract presentation of landscape as a thing 'felt' rather than 'seen'. Moreover this sense of a landscape experienced through atmosphere and weather resolved itself in work that was graphically less descriptive, more 'simple' as it were, but intellectually and emotionally more complex. The use of a reduced palette of white and of pale grey began to create a 'zen' like quality in the painting and so a mood that was abstracted, contemplative and mysterious. In some ways, then, a painting like *Weathering* is less about looking outwards than it is concerned with looking inwards. In this manner it is reflective of a personal development and a unique sense of lived experience. Indeed the very title seems to refer to the condition of living, growing, changing and aging that is the fundamental aspect of human experience.

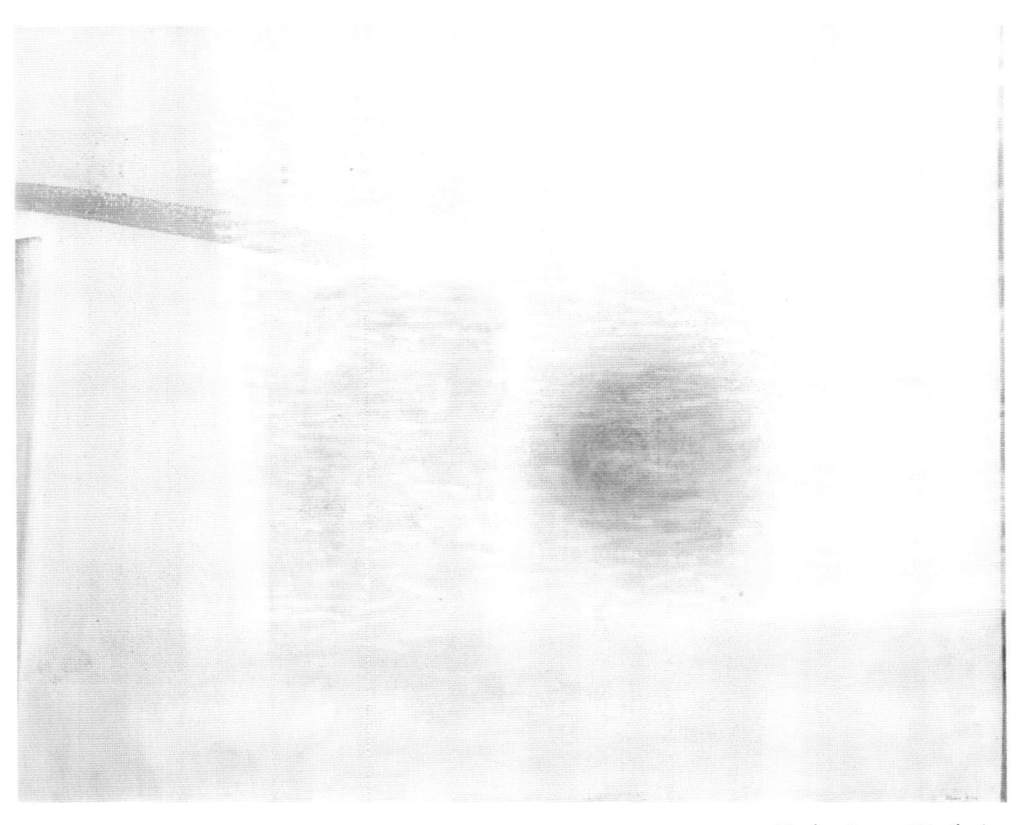

Marian Leven, *Weathering*

GLEN ONWIN, *Geevor Ortus*

The concern with change, and with process, has been a feature of the work of Glen Onwin (b.1947). Born in Edinburgh, and having both trained and taught at Edinburgh College of Art, he was elected an academician in 2010 on the presentation of the complex abstract work *Geevor Ortus* as his diploma piece. *Geevor Ortus* is a work in four parts that originated from a large installation titled 'Blood of the Pelican' that was created in the Geevor Tin Mine in Cornwall during 1997. This site-specific installation was fashioned in the abandoned 'shaking-shed' of the redundant mine. The original function of the 'shaking-shed' had been to separate the ore from the mined material and this process naturally generated coloured liquids. In a multi-dimension and multi-media project Onwin employed assistants to mix coloured compounds in shallow diamond-shaped vats. These viscose compounds echoed the tints of mined ores, and so; coal dust: black, china clay: white, tin ore dust: red, pottery clay: yellow.

In some ways this was a reflection of the activities of mining and the characteristics of natural materials, but the project was altogether more complex than this outline for it was both wider and deeper. The symbol of the Pelican, the association with the 'Ortus', and the loaded symbolism of the four chosen colours all provide pathways into myth and to alchemy. Equally Onwin has sited his interest in natural sciences and in the materials of creation; both the physical substances of creation and metaphysical dimensions of

materialisation. *Geevor Ortus* then represents a kind of meditation, or experiment, on the theme of transformation. However, Onwin has commented upon the making of the work: 'I made oil paint from the four ground materials... I then incorporated the paint into micro crystalline wax which I applied to the canvas on plywood board surfaces; black, white, red, yellow. The work... is made by coating the canvas mounted on board panels with pigments let into molten paraffin wax... The surface then has a solution of concentrated brine NaCl (sodium chloride) applied by pouring. This solution of common salt and water is then allowed to evaporate – the surface forms that are created by this process are an element of complete chance...' (RSA archive). And here the physical, the scientific, and the imaginative qualities of this kind of creative experiment are most fully realised.

Geevor Ortus, then, is remarkable series of images, an elusive and nuanced reflection on processes of material change. But it is also a larger contemplation on the materiality of the natural world, a materiality governed by laws and by chance yet embodying a striking metaphysics.

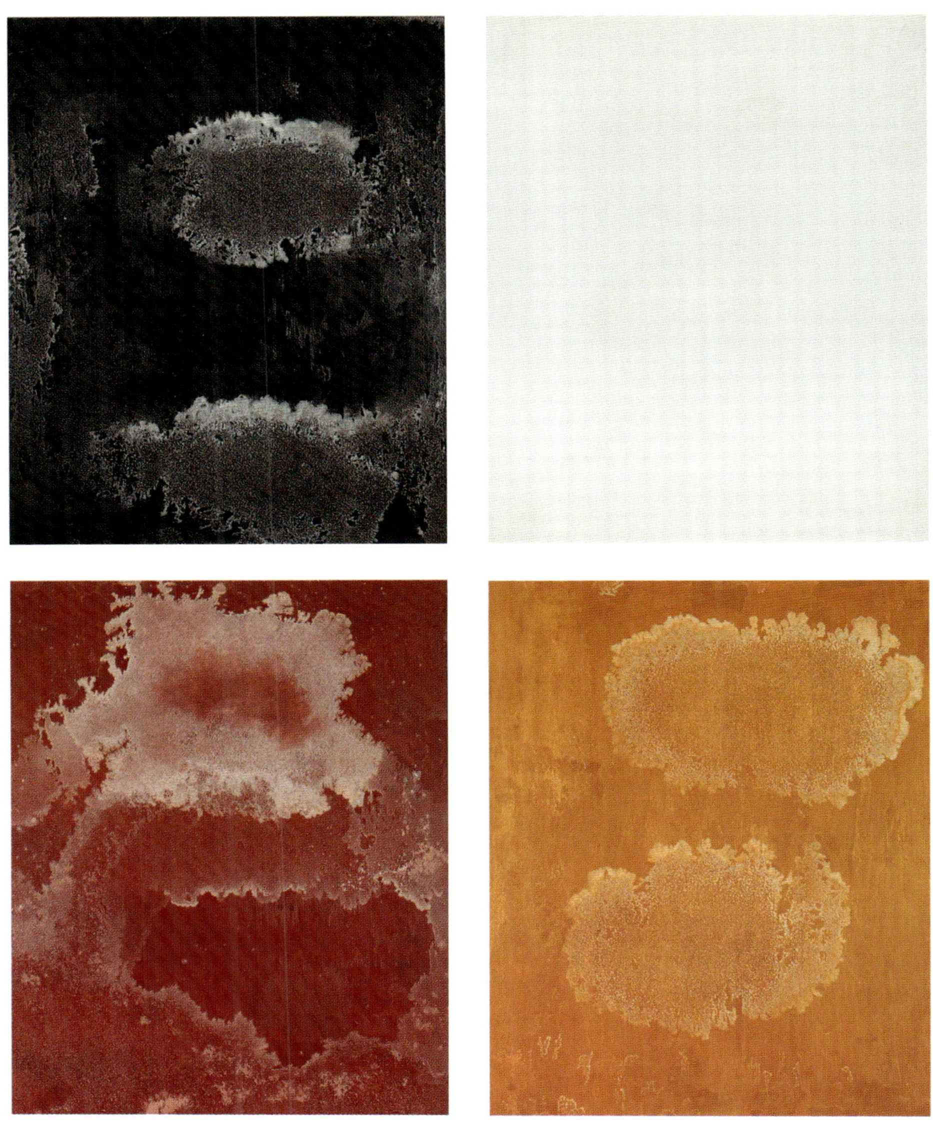

Glen Onwin, *Geevor Ortus (quadtych)*

GARETH FISHER, *Crystalobite*

The idea of chance, the notion of creative alchemy, and a concern for the nature of materials, is also a feature of Gareth Fisher's (b.1951) diploma piece. *Crystalobite*, submitted as a diploma work in 2005, is a delicate sculptural work created in plaster. Trained at Edinburgh College of Art, Fisher is fascinated by the British sculptural tradition and particularly the 'geometry of fear' sculptors of the 1950s and 1960s. Equally, the qualities of the 'Surrealist object' and a working method involving spontaneity and chance inform his practice. But *Crystalobite* is clearly more than the sum of these sources and is near unique as a sculptural presentation within the academy's collection.

Fisher is currently Professor of Sculpture at Duncan of Jordanstone College of Art in Dundee and the genesis of this work follows from the closure of the ceramics department within the college. Fisher occupied the abandoned space and was confronted with the 'glaze room'; an area that contained compounds and chemicals used to colour the clay objects. Crystalobite was one of the many oxides used in the process of glazing ceramics, along with Zirconium, Barium, Strontium, and others. Fisher began to mix these compounds with plaster and these amalgams would add colour and texture to the material. Working around a clay armature – subsequently removed – Fisher would generate aggregates from the poured, set and compound plaster material to create delicate and organic sculptural objects that responded to the material and to a larger sense of association in the form.

Crystalobite, then, is part of a 'Glaze Room Series' of works but subtly references the idea of the 'crown of thorns'. Hence, the rough circular base to the work, the thorn-like shape in the lower section, and the fragile bulbous nodule attached to the perpendicular spine. The sense of a vaguely menacing 'feel' to the work is palpable where the thorn implies puncture and the bulbous node appears ready to rupture. Indeed the notion of an object that is delicate and fragile to the point of fragmentation and collapse connotes an intuition that subtly references visions of mortality.

As a sculptural object this work is near unique within the diploma collection of the academy. The material is unconventional and friable. The plinth for the work is a simple flat platform: here in a pinkish-red colour designed to complement the discreet pink and green tones that the glaze oxides have imparted to the plaster. The object itself appears 'provisional' for being neither 'traditional' nor orthodox it exists as a contingent form open to varieties of meaning and inter-pretation. Simultaneously *Crystalobite* offers a fascinating intervention and challenge within the institution of the academy, and one that is relevant to the changing nature of creative practice.

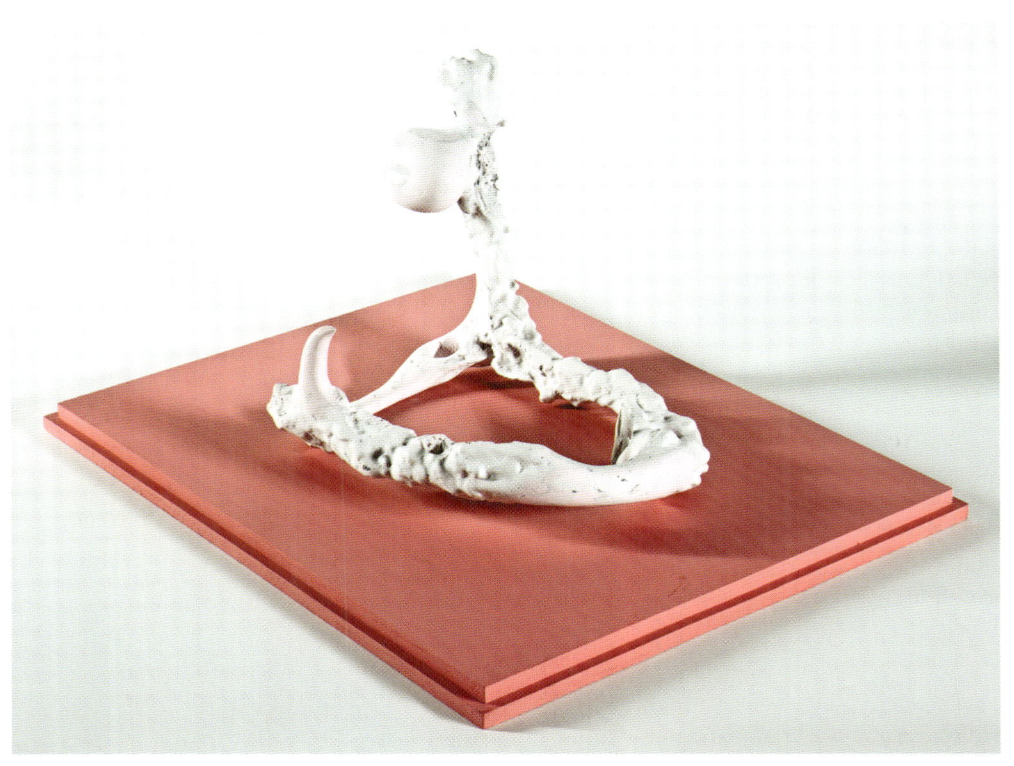

Gareth Fisher, *Crystalobite*

RONALD FORBES, *Diana Surprised by Actaeon*

The subject of transformation, magical change and metamorphosis is reprised in the diploma work of Ronald Forbes (b.1947). His *Diana Surprised by Actaeon*, submitted after his election to the academy in 2005, is a contemporary revisualization of the renowned classical subject. Diana, the Roman pagan goddess – a virgin deity of woodland and the hunt, a symbolic divinity also related to the moon – is surprised by Actaeon who is hunting with his hounds. She is naked and attended by her nymphs while bathing in a forest pool. Actaeon has seen her nakedness and, in punishment for this transgression, the goddess transforms him into a stag whereupon the hunter is set upon by his own hounds.

Forbes has, in his diploma work, presented a transformative imagining of one of the finest works in the collection of the Scottish National Gallery, Titian's *Diana and Actaeon* of 1556–9. Titian's glorious painting, one of seven works he based on tales from Ovid's 'Metamorphoses', has hung alongside the accompanying *Diana and Callisto* in the Scottish National Gallery, adjacent to the Royal Scottish Academy building on The Mound, for the whole of the post-war period. It has, naturally, been an inspiration for generations of artists and remains a jewel in Scotland's rich visual heritage.

In *Diana Surprised by Actaeon* Forbes has recognised the esteem of Titian's work but the motifs and stylisation of the painting is completely bound to his personal language. Trained at Edinburgh College of Art in the mid-1960s Forbes is concerned with looking and 'seeing' – that leitmotif of the Diana and Actaeon myth – but not in the academic or 'painterly' sense of these procedures. Rather, his work has explored a philosophical discourse that speculates on the nature of reality, recognises the discontinuity in spatial and temporal dimensions, offers a series of counterpoints relating to the physical and the immaterial, and traverses the borderline between illusion and allusion. Moreover he explores these themes through a subtle technique that conjures with aspects of *trompe l'oeil* painting, reimagines the procedures of collage, and reinvents aspects of modernist and postmodern practice. These are all features of his *Diana Surprised by Actaeon* where the fractured landscape presents a panorama of blue sky and hills, lush foliage, exotic flowers, and earthwork. This is the setting for the hunter and the nymphs who act out their drama in contemporary corsetry and as if disjointed mannequins. The narrative of the myth is echoed within the work where shades of hunter and stag are repeated in the painting. The sense of a collaged and discontinuous representation is accented by the breaks in visual sequence that intimate an accumulation of fissures in time and in space. Equally, the ghost of an axiomatic drawing, a box or frame, complicates any reading of the painting as a simple account or description of the myth. In fact the work is homage to the classical tradition, in some degree to 'academicism', and a recognition of the complex visual world – the dislocated, impermanent, 'unreal' world – of the present.

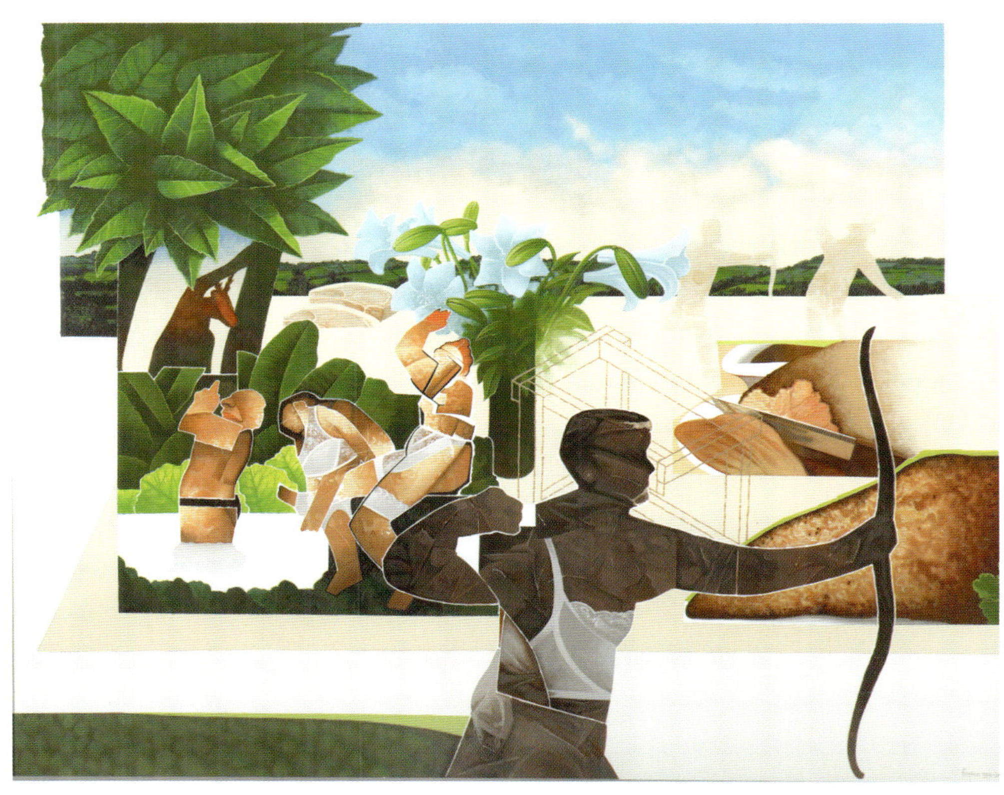

Ronald Forbes, *Diana Surprised by Actaeon*

Whereas Ronald Forbes has sourced his diploma work in classical mythology the narratives and associations of the Judeo-Christian bible still have some resonance in recent academic practice. As it occurs this is most evident in the field of printmaking.

When Willie Rodger (b.1930) was elected an associate academician he was the first individual to be voted to the institution as a dedicated printmaker. Certainly the academy had, in its early years, elected engravers as associate members with the first being the eminent William Home Lizars who was involved with the founding of the academy in 1826, and was an 'engraver and painter'. Willie Rodger, however, has built a reputation working in woodcut and linocut and these techniques are both present in *Temptation and Fall*, his diploma submission of 2005. Rodger's subjects have been wide-ranging and accessible with a taste for the vernacular and the everyday. In *Temptation and Fall* the subject, from the Book of Genesis, relates to Eve and the apple, and evidently the arm of Eve, having collected the apple, resonates in its snake-like form.

The significance of printmaking to contemporary practice has been further acknowledged in the election of Stuart Duffin (b.1959), again in 2005. His diploma work *Hope in Wisdom, Hope in Darkness* is a mezzotint. This technique, based on engraving but technically and physically demanding, allows for a deep, dark and dramatic final image. Also an image that lends itself to closely worked draughtsmanship. *Hope in Wisdom, Hope in Darkness* relates to Duffin's period of work in the Jerusalem Print Workshop in Israel during 2006. The artist has commented that: 'the street sign on the wall, in the mezzotint, is one at the foot of the stairs at the Jerusalem Print Workshop... The sign written in English, Arabic and Hebrew represents, for me, the three religions there (Christianity, Islam and Judaism). The bullet holes are from around my studio window. I have juxtaposed contemporary graffiti with the ancient "Lamentations of Jeremiah" '. And so the print reflects upon current events relating to the Abrahamic religions.

In truth printmaking has been a core practice amongst Scottish artists with the high-water-mark evidenced in the work of James McBey, David Young Cameron (RSA 1918), Ernest Stephen Lumsden (RSA 1934), David MacBeth Sutherland (RSA 1937) and Iain Macnab, all of who turned to printmaking during the economic chills of the early 20th century. Some of these eminent figures would be elected academicians, but entirely for their skill as painters. In recent years a new generation of printmakers, and thriving print studios, have become a feature of the Scottish art world and so the academy has recognised this in its elections and its diploma works.

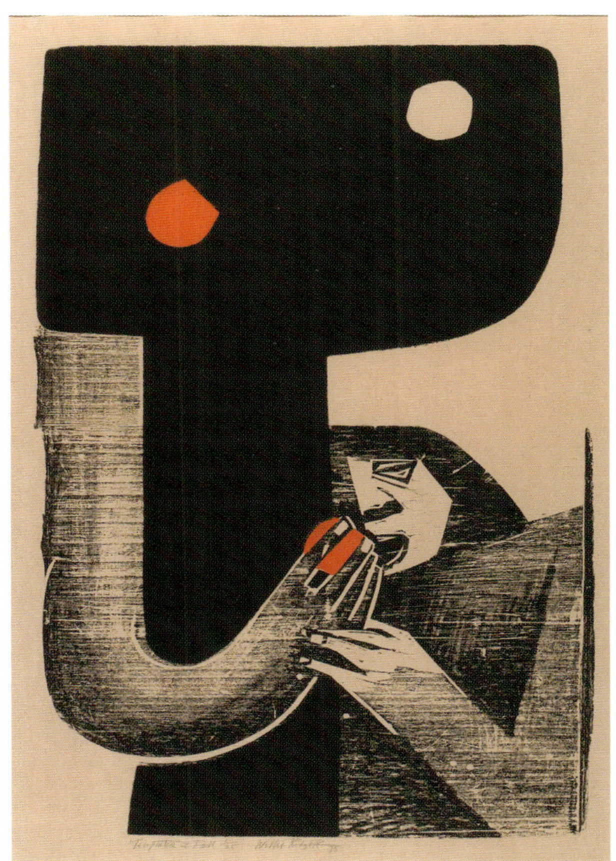

Willie Rodger, *Temptation and Fall*

Stuart Duffin, *Hope in Wisdom, Hope in Darkness*

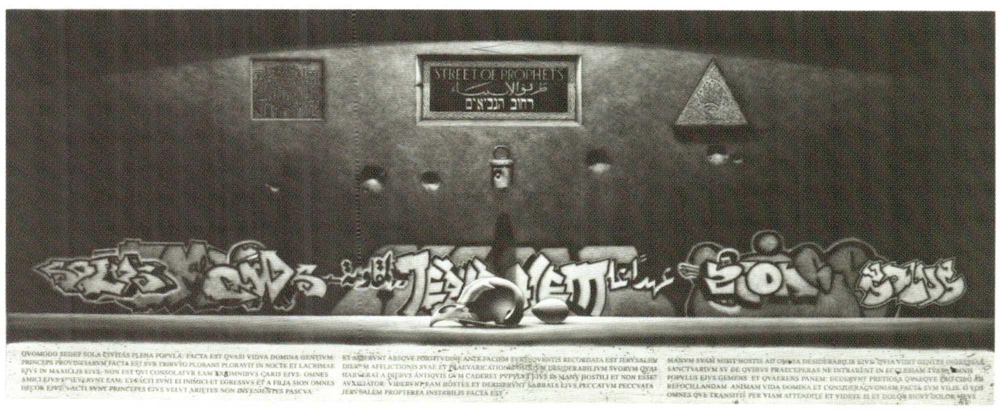

JOHN BYRNE, *Smoking Beach Boy*

The sense of a revitalisation of the academy in the new millennium is evident in a refreshed election procedure that has enabled greater inclusivity and diversity within the membership. In this event it is not simply new media that have been exhibited and welcomed within the academy walls but also multi-media, intermedia and neo-conceptual strategies. It might be argued that the future of the academy lies in recognising the variety and adventure of younger Scottish artists whose aspirations reach out towards the challenges of a 'fluid' and less orthodox understanding of the 'work of art'.

In some degree this was acknowledged with the election of John Byrne (b.1940) to the academy in 2007. Byrne is a significant individual because he was, for some years, a marginal or 'outsider' figure in the Scottish art world. Moreover, he consistently traversed the boundaries between artist, printmaker, illustrator, designer, and, set and stage painter. Even more adventurously he has made a reputation as an award-winning writer of plays and an eminent designer and producer of these works. In many ways his very persona has become a work of art; a performance piece.

From a varied background Byrne became a student at Glasgow School of Art in 1958. An acclaimed draughtsman he worked as a graphic designer before inventing the 'naïve' painter 'Patrick' and finding the work of this doppelganger celebrated during the late 1960s and '70s. Indeed as 'Patrick' he became celebrated for his album cover graphics for the major performers of the period. Following a landmark exhibition of his work at the Third Eye Centre in Glasgow in 1975 he began a career as a playwright and had international success with 'The Slab Boys' in 1978 and later with the television serial 'Tutti-Frutti' in 1988. Continually designing and drawing in this period he would return to exhibiting his work in the 1990s, to great acclaim. All of this amounts to a rich and varied career and one that does not quite meld with the conventional pathway of professional painter. But it does recognise the kind of multi-dimension, intermedia and context-based practice of contemporary art. In this manner Byrne is something of a progenitor for the new generation of artists.

His diploma work, *Smoking Beach Boy*, does signal his core activity as graphic artist and his concern with figure and narrative. An oil on hardboard, a large and impressive triptych, the work is redolent of a signature style that engages its subject with wit and even an element of jest. This is characteristic of Byrne's approach but embodies, also, a subtle allusion to the tragic, or at least the tragi-comic, in the imagery. Here, and elsewhere in the artist's work, the haunted 'outsider' persona reflects a pathos of misfortune and heartbreak.

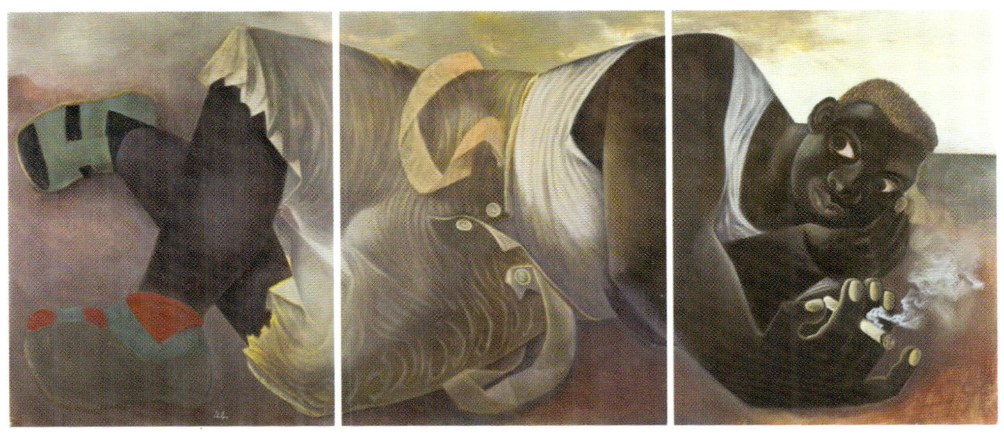

John Byrne, *Smoking Beach Boy* (triptych)

ARTHUR WATSON, *Arkival*

The development of contemporary art practice, and particularly the sense of the artwork as an open, fluid, contingent and freely negotiated forum for observation and understanding is fully expressed in the diploma piece submitted by the current President of the academy, Arthur Watson (b.1951).

Watson was elected a full academician in 2005 and was made the 21st President of the Royal Scottish Academy in 2012. Trained at Gray's School of Art in Aberdeen, and a founder of the renowned Peacock Printmakers Workshop in the city, Watson has sourced much of his work in the folk traditions of the north-east. Furthermore, he has expanded this to an interest in non-material cultures; the oral tradition, the nature of language, and ephemeral or transient phenomenon and imagery. The intellectual and creative ambition of this approach has been realised in the complex multi-dimensional projects he has undertaken, many of these being international collaborations.

The diploma piece *Arkival* is a unique contribution to the academy's diploma collection and fully represents Watson's eclectic and challenging approach. Sandy Wood, the assistant curator at the academy, has written that: '(with)… *Arkival* we will receive a work that will truly change the blueprint of the Diploma Collection… (for)… *Arkival* will consist of three exhibition crates containing material that has the capacity to afford creative and adaptable installation options' (Wood 8). In fact Watson is presenting a kind of personal 'archive' to the collection, the fullest expression of his studio practice since 1975 and a document of his creative experiments: it is composed of drawings, objects, sculptures, multiples, catalogues and every variety of related material all packed into crates that may be used as pediments for display. However, this archive acknowledges not only the materials of his working methods, thought processes and output, but references conceptual and contemporary practice. That is, *Arkival* may be framed within the paradigm of installation, exhibition and display, cataloguing, and the negotiated relationship between artist and audience. Consequently *Arkival* is a reflection upon the nature of a 'collection' as a thing in itself, and, as a milieu for representation, memory and association. Moreover, it implies a context for a revitalised social mediation between the artist and public through the potential for variable presentations.

In many ways the ambition of *Arkival* is a template for the diploma collection of the future; experimental, challenging, diverse, mutable, collaborative, and open to every degree of creative exploration. A treasure-chest of visually exciting, and thought-provoking, artwork.

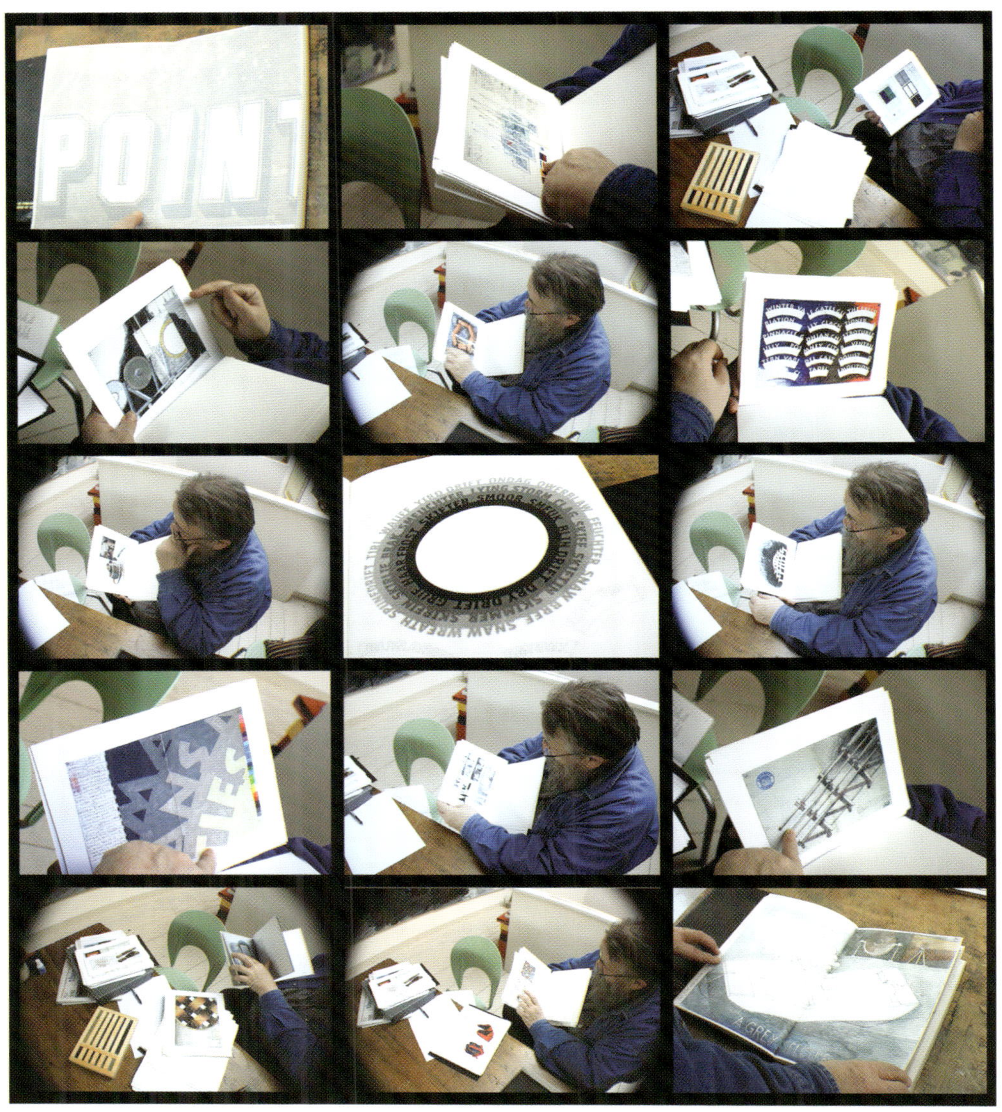

Arthur Watson, *Arkival*

The future of the Royal Scottish Academy is, in many ways, the future of Scottish art and art in Scotland. Certainly Scottish art has had, and continues to have, an international role and profile. From the new visions of post-Enlightenment Edinburgh, through the Impressionism of the 'Glasgow Boys', and encompassing the Symbolist and Colourist experiments of the 20th century, Scottish art has engaged with aspects of modernism and modernity. More recently this dynamic has been sustained in the success of the 'New Glasgow Boys' during the 1980s, through to the celebrations surrounding the 'neo-conceptualists' in the 1990s, and on to the exhaustive list of Turner Prize winning artists from Scotland. The academy, in its history, has been a vital part of that international role, freely exhibiting the newest and the best of modern art and respecting the multi-dimensional approaches of contemporary art.

While this kind of international profile is fundamental to the vitality of Scotland's art it is the dynamism and radical ambition of Scotland's art institutions that will sustain the visual culture into the future. Patently, the economic and financial base of Scotland's art-world is limited. In this respect dealers and brokers in art are under pressure and public funding for the visual arts is severely limited. The impact of these conditions on national galleries and related institutions results in a constrained exhibitions policy and restricted monies for new acquisitions. In fact it was precisely these conditions that forced younger artists, during the 1990s, to produce self-generated, or artist-run, exhibitions in unconventional spaces: these were frequently sited in bed-sitting rooms, or, as in the case of the landmark 'Windfall 1991' exhibition of younger multi-media contemporary artists, in reassigned buildings like the Seaman's Mission Hall in Glasgow. The academy, however, remains an independent and artist-run organisation; in this sense it exists outside of the constrained public sphere, and the commercially dependent private dealerships. Fundamentally, it is created by Scottish artists to promote Scottish art, and it is limited only by the vision and ambition of its members. The momentum within this institution, from at least the dawn of the new millennium, has been towards an open, diverse, inclusive, challenging and forward-thinking programme. This agenda recognises the value of established art forms while embracing the rigour and potential of new media and contemporary practice. In fact acknowledging the global dynamic of new art and visual culture within the context of a 'local' paradigm.

The Royal Scottish Academy of Art and Architecture, then, is far from being an establishment institution and a bastion of tradition. Rather, it is an artists' cooperative created and shaped by its members. Increasingly open to every range of art and artist it can become the forum for vigorous debate, challenging artwork and radical initiative. The Diploma Collection sits at its heart as evidence of its history, and the history of Scottish art. Like that history the works displayed here are sometimes conventional, occasionally idiosyncratic, and often exceptional. If Scottish art is to flourish in the coming decades it is the last of these adjectives that should inform the model for the future, and it is the academy that has the potential to realise this prospect.

BIBLIOGRAPHY

WORKS CITED IN THE TEXT

James Caw: *Scottish Painting: Past and Present 1620–1908* (Edinburgh: T. C. and E. C. Jack, 1908).

Esme Gordon: *The Royal Scottish Academy 1826–1976* (Edinburgh: Charles Skilton Ltd, 1976).

Keith Hartley: *Scottish Art since 1900* (Edinburgh: Scottish National Galleries, 1989).

Janice Helland: *Professional Women Painters in Nineteenth-Century Scotland*, (Ashgate Press, Aldershot, 2000).

Clare Henry, et.al.: *The Vigorous Imagination – New Scottish Art* (Edinburgh: National Galleries of Scotland, 1987).

Jake Kemplay: *The Edinburgh Group*, catalogue, (Edinburgh: City Arts Centre, 1983).

Murdo Macdonald, Joanna Soden, Lesley Lindsay, Will Maclean (eds): *Highland Art: a Window to the West*, (Edinburgh: RSA 2008).

William D. Mackay: *The Scottish School of Painting* (London: Duckworth & Co, 1906).

Duncan Macmillan: *Painting in Scotland: the Golden Age* (Oxford: Phaidon Press, 1986).

Duncan Macmillan: *Scottish Art in the 20th Century* (Edinburgh: Mainstream, 1995).

Fiona MacSporran: *Edward Arthur Walton* (Glasgow: Foulis Archive Press, 1987).

Alexander Moffat: 'Telling Stories: a New Figuration in Glasgow 1980–1985' in *New Image Glasgow*, catalogue, (Glasgow: Third Eye Centre, 1985).

John Morrison: *Painting the Nation: Identity and Nationalism in Scottish Painting 1800–1920* (Edinburgh: Edinburgh University Press, 2003).

Belinda Morse: *A Woman of Design, A Man of Passion: the Pioneering McIans* (Lewes: The Book Guild, 2001).

Royal Scottish Academy: Constitution and Laws, catalogues, and archive.

Joanna Soden, notes on the Collection, personal correspondence.

John Tonge: *The Arts of Scotland* (London: Kegan Paul, Trench, Trubner & Co, 1938).

Sandy Wood: 'Arkival: a living, evolving artwork for the Royal Scottish Academy Collections' *Scottish Society of Art History: Newsletter No.39*, Spring 2012. (available at: www.ssah.org.uk).

RELATED WORKS

Roger Billcliffe: *The Glasgow Boys: the Glasgow School of Painting 1875–1895* (London: Frances Lincoln, 2008).

Patrick Bourne: *Anne Redpath 1895–1965. Her life and work* (Edinburgh & London, Bourne Fine Art & The Portland Gallery 1989).

George Bruce: *Anne Redpath, Modern Scottish Painters series, no 1* (Edinburgh: University of Edinburgh 1974).

Robert Brydall: *Art in Scotland: its origins and progress* (Edinburgh: Blackwood, 1889).

William Buchanan: *Joan Eardley. Modern Scottish Painters series, no 5* (Edinburgh: University of Edinburgh, 1976).

Jude Burkhauser (ed): *The Glasgow Girls: Women in Art and Design 1880–1920*, (Edinburgh: Canongate Books Ltd., 1990).

Mungo Campbell: *David Scott 1806–1849, Scottish Masters series II* (Edinburgh: National Galleries of Scotland, 1990.

James Caw: *Sir James Guthrie PRSA, LLD* (London: Macmillan & Co, 1932).

Richard Cork et. al: *Kate Whiteford: land drawings, installations, excavations* (London: Black Dog, 2008).

Stanley Cursiter: *Peploe. An intimate memoir of an artist and of his work* (London & Edinburgh: Thomas Nelson & Sons, 1947).

Rafael C. Denis and Colin Trodd: *Art and the academy in the nineteenth century* (Manchester: Manchester University Press, 2000).

Maria Devaney: *Joseph Denovan Adam RSA, RSW (1841–1896): Mountain, Meadow, Moss and Moor* (Stirling: Smith Art Gallery & Museum, 1996).

T Elder Dickson: *W G Gillies. Modern Scottish Painters series, no 2* (Edinburgh: University of Edinburgh, 1974).

Lindsay Errington: *Master Class: Robert Scott Lauder and his Pupils* (Edinburgh: National Galleries of Scotland, 1983).

Sidney Gilpin: *Sam Bough RSA, some account of his life and works* (London: George Bell & Sons, 1905).

Lindsay Gordon: *Robin Philipson, Modern Scottish Painters series, no 6* (Edinburgh: University of Edinburgh, 1976).

Bill Hare: *Contemporary Painting in Scotland* (Tortola: Craftsman House, 1999).

Robert Hewison: *John Byrne* (London: Lund Humphries, 2011).

Peter Hill: *Ronald Forbes (mind) games Paintings: Film* (Dundee: University of Abertay 2005).

Gil & Pat Hitchon: *Sam Bough RSA: The Rivers in Bohemia* (Lewes: The Book Guild, 1998)

Christopher Hussey: *The Work of Sir Robert Lorimer* (Country Life 1931).

David and Fracina Irwin: *Scottish Painters at Home and Abroad 1700–1900* (London: Faber and Faber, 1975).

Victoria Keller: *Robin Philipson 1916–1992* (Edinburgh: National Galleries of Scotland, 1999).

Jake Kemplay: *John Duncan: a Scottish Symbolist* (San Francisco: Pomegranate Artbooks, 1994).

James Lawson: *Calum Colvin: Sacred and Profane* (Edinburgh: National Galleries of Scotland, 1998).

Maria Lind and John Calcutt: *Here + Now: Scottish Art 1990–2001* (Dundee: Dundee Contemporary Arts, 2001).

Phillip Long: *Anne Redpath 1895–1965* (Edinburgh: National Galleries of Scotland, 1996).

Philip Long: *Elizabeth Blackadder* (London: Yale University Press, 2011).

Philip Long: *John Maxwell 1905–1962* (Edinburgh: National Galleries of Scotland, 1998).

Philip Long and Elizabeth Cumming: *The Scottish Colourists* (Edinburgh: Mainstream, 2000).

David McClure: *John Maxwell. Modern Scottish Painters series, no 4* (Edinburgh: University of Edinburgh, 1976).

Murdo Macdonald: *Scottish Art* (London: Thames and Hudson, 2000).

Duncan Macmillan: *Scottish Art 1460–2000* (Edinburgh: Mainstream, 2000).

Duncan Macmillan: *Symbols of Survival: the art of Will Maclean* (Edinburgh: Mainstream, 1992).

Duncan Macmillan and Murdo Macdonald: *Scotland's Art* (Edinburgh: City of Edinburgh Museums, 1990).

Jennifer Melville: *Pittendrigh Macgillivray* (Aberdeen: Aberdeen Art Gallery & Museums 1988).

Neil Mulholland: *The Cultural Devolution: Art in Britain in the late 20th Century*, (London: Ashgate Publishing, 2003).

M. H. Noel-Paton & J. P. Campbell: *Noel Paton 1821–1901* (Edinburgh: Ramsay Head Press 1990).

Tom Normand: *Scottish Photography: a history* (Edinburgh, Luath Press, 2007).

Tom Normand: *The Modern Scot: Modernism and Nationalism in Scottish Art 1928–1955* (Aldershot: Ashgate Press, 2000).

Cordelia Oliver: *James Cowie, Modern Scottish Painters series, no 7* (Edinburgh: University of Edinburgh 1980).

Cordelia Oliver: *Joan Eardley RSA* (Edinburgh: Mainstream, 1988).

Andrew Patrizio: *Contemporary Sculpture in Scotland* (Amsterdam: Craftsman House, 1999).

Fiona Pearson: *Joan Eardley* (Edinburgh: National Galleries of Scotland 2007).

Fiona Pearson: *Vision and Virtue: Sculpture and Scotland 1540–1990* (Edinburgh: National Galleries of Scotland, 1991).

Guy Peploe: *S J Peploe 1871–1935* (Edinburgh: Mainstream, 2000).

Alan Riach and Alexander Moffat: *Arts of Resistance: Poets, Portraits and Landscapes in Modern Scotland* (Edinburgh: Luath Press, 2009).

Craig Richardson: *Scottish Art since 1960: historical reflections and contemporary overviews* (Burlington VT: Ashgate, 2010).

Frank Rinder and William D. MacKay: *The Royal Scottish Academy 1826–1916* (Glasgow: James Maclehose and Sons, 1917).

Joe Rock: *Thomas Hamilton Architect 1784–1858* (Edinburgh 1984).

Peter Savage: *Lorimer and the Edinburgh craft designer* (Edinburgh: Paul Harris 1980).

William B Scott: *Memoir of David Scott RSA, containing his journal in Italy, notes on art and other papers* (Edinburgh: Adam & Charles Black, 1850).

W. Gordon Smith: *Philipson. A biography of Sir Robin Philipson* (Edinburgh: Atelier Books, 1995).

W. Gordon Smith: *William Gillies: a very still life* (Edinburgh: Atelier Books, 1991).

Joanna Soden: *Paintings from the Diploma Collection of the Royal Scottish Academy, catalogue*, (Edinburgh: RSA 1993).

Joanna Soden & Victoria Keller: *William Gillies* (Edinburgh: Canongate 1998).

Arthur Watson (ed.): *Joyce Cairns: War Tourist* (Aberdeen: Aberdeen Art Gallery, 2006).

W Harvey Wood: *William MacTaggart. Modern Scottish Painters series, no 3* (Edinburgh: University of Edinburgh, 1974).

Scottish Photography: A History

Tom Normand
ISBN 978-1-906307-07-3 HBK £29.99

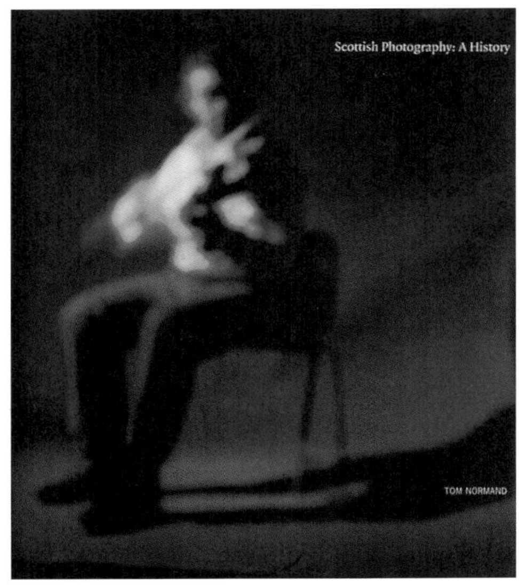

What served in the place of the photograph before the camera's invention? The expected answer is engraving, the drawing, the painting. The more revealing answer might be memory. What photographs do out there in space was previously done within reflection.
JOHN BERGER

Scotland has made a rich contribution to the art of photography throughout the world. Beginning with the stellar images of Hill and Adamson, and progressing through the vivid landscape and documentary traditions, Scottish photographers have created a resonant and dramatic photographic culture. Today, the radical experimentation of contemporary Scottish photographers continues to push photography to new heights, and towards assuring its own status as an art form.

Normand examines the photograph as an object, a form of documentary, and as a memorial; and the ways in which the Scottish connection has altered or defined these forms. The history of photography from Scotland has never before been given its proper place in world photography; nor has it been told so well.

A photograph is distilled, charmed, disturbing, intense, and ethereal correspondence with the world: a talisman empowered by the ineluctable mystery of the visual.
TOM NORMAND

A stimulating, remarkably comprehensive account of a fascinating subject.
NORTHERN EXPOSURE

As Others See Us: Personal views on the life and works of Robert Burns

Portraits by Tricia Malley and Ross Gillespie
ISBN 978-1906817-06-0 HBK £9.99
ISBN 978-1906817-52-7 PBK £7.99

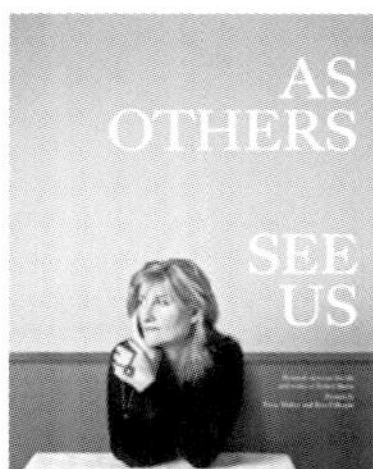

As Others See Us is a unique, innovative photographic project produced by award-winning photographers Tricia Malley and Ross Gillespie

The challenge here was to capture not only each individual sitter's character but also try to convey something of the essence of his or her favourite Burns poem in a single portrait. The work of Robert Burns can be quite abstract or highly visual... sometimes both. Inspiration came from being reminded of the works of Burns, being introduced to new pieces and seeing them through the eyes of the sitters.

As we discovered during the time spent on this project, Robert Burns is just as relevant, entertaining and inspiring today as he was 250 years ago.

TRICIA MALLEY & ROSS GILLESPIE

Arts of Resistance: Poets, Portraits and Landscapes of Modern Scotland

Alan Riach and Alexander Moffat,
with contributions by Linda MacDonald-Lewis
ISBN 978-1-906817-18-3 PBK £16.99

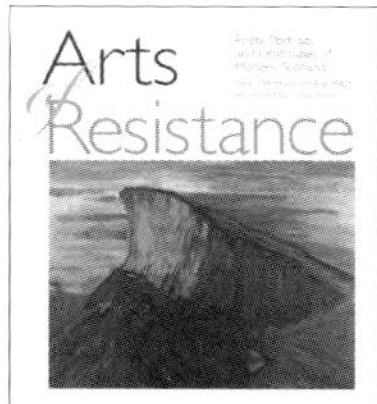

The role of art in the modern world is to challenge and provoke, to resist stagnation and to question complacency. All art, whether poetry, painting or prose, represents and interprets the world. Its purpose is to bring new perspectives to what life can be.
ALEXANDER MOFFAT and ALAN RIACH

Arts of Resistance is an original exploration that extends beyond the arts into the context of politics and political change. In three wide-ranging exchanges prompted by American blues singer Linda MacDonald-Lewis, artist Alexander Moffat and poet Alan Riach, discuss cultural, political and artistic movements, the role of the artist in society and the effect of environment on artists from all disciplines.

Highly illustrated with paintings and poems, Arts of Resistance is a beautifully produced book providing facts and controversial opinions.

... an inspiration, a revelation and education as to the extraordinary richness and organic cohesion of twentieth-century Scottish culture, full of intellectual adventure... a landmark book.
TIMES LITERARY SUPPLEMENT

Details of these and other books published by Luath Press can be found at:
www.luath.co.uk

Luath Press Limited

committed to publishing well written books worth reading

LUATH PRESS takes its name from Robert Burns, whose little collie Luath (*Gael.,* swift or nimble) tripped up Jean Armour at a wedding and gave him the chance to speak to the woman who was to be his wife and the abiding love of his life. Burns called one of 'The Twa Dogs' Luath after Cuchullin's hunting dog in Ossian's *Fingal*. Luath Press was established in 1981 in the heart of Burns country, and is now based a few steps up the road from Burns' first lodgings on Edinburgh's Royal Mile.
Luath offers you distinctive writing with a hint of unexpected pleasures.

Most bookshops in the UK, the US, Canada, Australia, New Zealand and parts of Europe either carry our books in stock or can order them for you. To order direct from us, please send a £sterling cheque, postal order, international money order or your credit card details (number, address of cardholder and expiry date) to us at the address below. Please add post and packing as follows: UK – £1.00 per delivery address; overseas surface mail – £2.50 per delivery address; overseas airmail – £3.50 for the first book to each delivery address, plus £1.00 for each additional book by airmail to the same address. If your order is a gift, we will happily enclose your card or message at no extra charge.

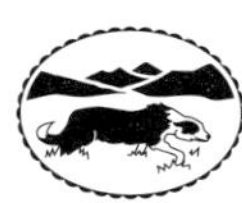

Luath Press Limited
543/2 Castlehill
The Royal Mile
Edinburgh EH1 2ND
Scotland
Telephone: 0131 225 4326 (24 hours)
Fax: 0131 225 4324
email: sales@luath.co.uk
Website: www.luath.co.uk

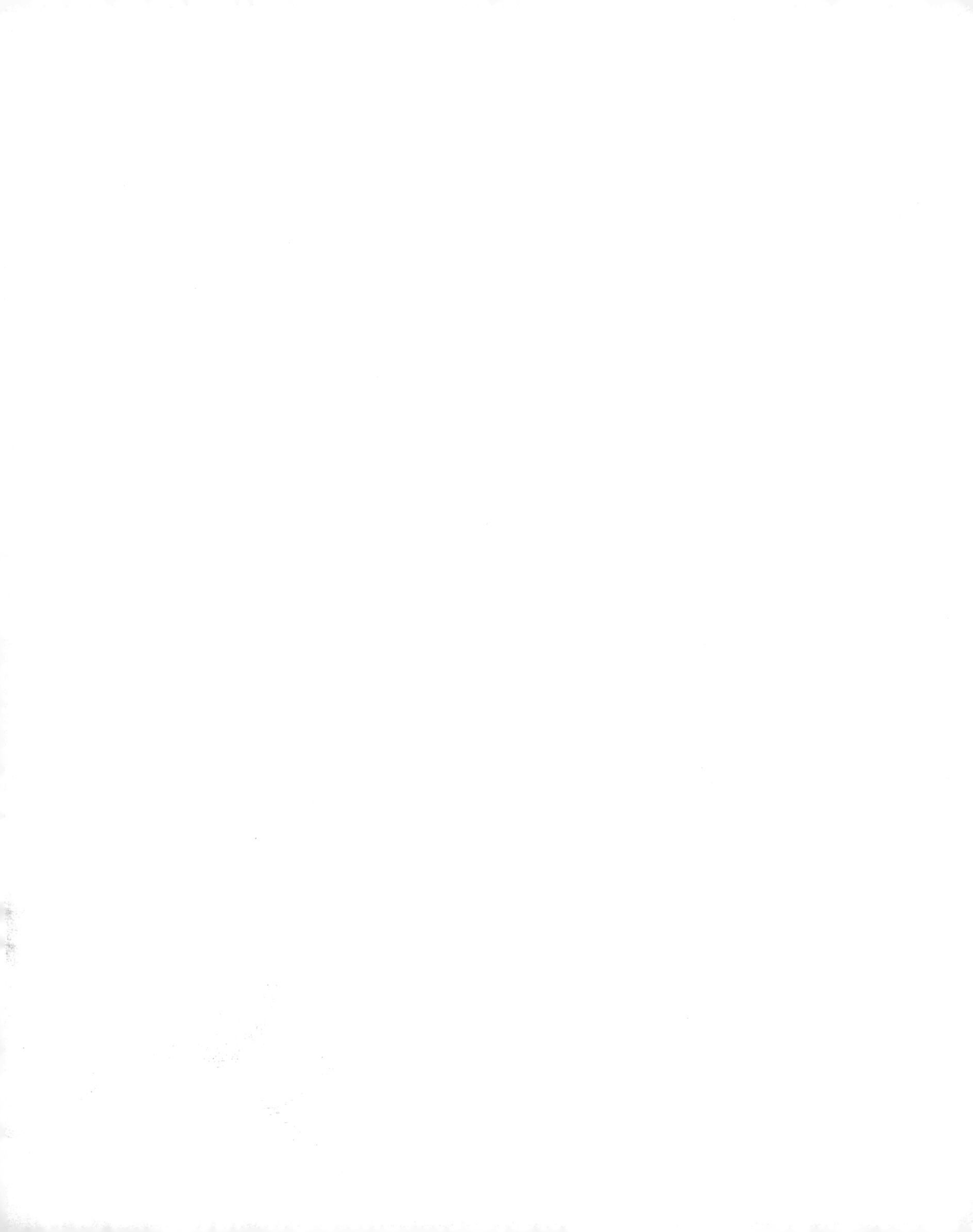